T5-BBW-922

RETAIL DECENTRALIZATION

RETAIL DECENTRALIZATION

by

Eli P. Cox

Professor of Marketing and
Director, Division of Research
Graduate School of Business Administration
Michigan State University

and

Leo G. Erickson

Professor of Marketing and
Director, Bureau of Business
and Economic Research
Graduate School of Business Administration
Michigan State University

1967

Bureau of Business and Economic Research
Division of Research
Graduate School of Business Administration
Michigan State University
East Lansing, Michigan

ACKNOWLEDGMENTS

We wish to acknowledge the contribution of several persons in preparing this study for publication.

Charles Van Tassel, Paul Larson, and Lynn Myers, all research assistants at the time in the Bureau of Business and Economic Research, Graduate School of Business Administration, Michigan State University, helped gather and organize the data. The Bureau's editors were quite helpful. Particular appreciation is due Esther Waite who did the final editing and preparation of the manuscript for publication. Any errors of fact or interpretation are the fault of one or more of those mentioned above.

Eli P. Cox
Leo G. Erickson
March, 1967

CONTENTS

LIST OF TABLES

CHAPTER I

INTRODUCTION

If there is any area in which marketers should have a unique competence it is the area of consumer demand. We are forced to admit, however, that we are still largely in the dark as to why consumers buy the items that they buy in the places that they do. Despite a wealth of data on consumption and despite improved techniques in motivation research, we still must conclude that we know very little about this most important economic activity. Indeed, as Kenneth Boulding has said in another context, the whole structure of economics has been weakened by a "general failure to appreciate the nature of consumption."[1]

Perhaps one facet of consumer demand--retail trade area determination--has gained more precision in marketing literature than has any other. The works of William J. Reilly[2] and Paul D. Converse[3] have made significant contributions in the understanding of retail trade flows. The generalizations resulting from the studies of these marketing pioneers have served both scholars and practitioners of marketing in good stead. In fact, the writers have used the formulations on occasions which have exceeded the limits imposed by both Reilly and Converse and have done so with good practical results.

Few areas of exploration are of more interest to marketing professionals than the flow of retail trade; its magnitude and direction of flow are determinants of the importance and the location of retail markets. These in turn influence the composition of wholesale networks and the location of manufacturing facilities to feed wholesale and retail markets. Furthermore, the structure designed to feed retail markets has considerable influence on the character of manufacturers and distributors of industrial goods. Thus in a consumer-directed system such as ours, the whole economy tends to orient itself toward retail markets and their efficient exploitation. Sometimes this orientation takes the form of product variation to fit the special needs of geographically dispersed retail concentrations, and sometimes it affects suppliers' strategy involving the decentralization of production and distribution facilities in order to reduce transportation costs and to be more competitive in distant markets.

The importance of a retailing center depends on the size and income of its population, the power of its institutions to attract people from the outside, and the relative drawing power of competing trading centers. Since all of these factors are variable, it is logical to assume that shifts in population, changes in income and its distribution, and changes in the quality of institutions affect the relative importance of competing retailing centers over time. It is also logical to assume that all those who make business decisions are interested in the changes that have taken place, and that those who plan are concerned with trends of retail concentration and decentralization.

Unfortunately, it is not possible to deal here with those studies that have come to be known conveniently under the general heading of "Reilly's Law." Phrased in the most general terms, the law tenders the proposition that, all else being equal, the ability of a city to attract customers from outside its boundaries is a function of the city's size (expressed in population).

Not only has marketing research indicated that Reilly's Law tends to work, but that it also has stood up under the test of logic. It is obvious that larger cities have more tendency than smaller ones to attract trade from greater distances. In addition to the retail structure of a major city offering the consumer a wider assortment of goods, many non-retailing attractions bring him there, where he is exposed to the shopping enticements which exist in such abundance.

Beginning in the 1930's, Reilly's Law captured the imagination of marketing men because it helped to explain the tremendous changes that were taking place in the nation's retail distribution pattern. The automobile had given the consumer a mobility that brought distant trading centers closer in time than local centers used to be. Furthermore, going to larger and more distant centers opened his eyes to the local centers' limitations in satisfying his new-found wants.

The result was obvious across the countryside. Small towns located within easy driving distance of larger cities practically disappeared. Retailer after retailer was forced out of business by dwindling trade, carrying local banks and other institutions with him.

Although there are insufficient retail sales data prior to 1929 to support such an assumption, it seems certain that retail activity concentrated in large population centers at a rapid rate during the second and third decades of this century. Increased consumer mobility was not the only factor at work to stimulate the flow of trade. Increasing cash incomes of non-metropolitan residents made possible the purchase of greater quantities of shopping and luxury goods, and their rising levels of education and sophistication seem to have directed the flow of trade toward the city.

Despite the fact that the forces which once caused trade to flow to larger centers are still present, perhaps to a greater degree than before, the relative magnitude of the flow has dwindled and this process of diminution appears to be continuing.

The purpose of this monograph is to extend the work of Reilly and Converse, and in doing so, we are attempting to say (however indirectly) something meaningful about trading areas. To make clear that our purpose is to elaborate on Reilly's Law and is not an attempt to refute it, it is helpful to state several observations made by Reilly and Converse in connection with their research. Such observations point up the consistency of the findings of this study with the earlier studies on retail trade flow.

First, Reilly stated in 1929:

But in connection with the centralization of markets for style goods, a noticeable reaction has already begun. The use of the automobile has resulted in such congestion in the downtown section of our larger cities that the inconveniences involved have tended to repel rather than to attract retail trade. [4]

Second, Reilly had always intended population to be a proxy variable as an attraction for trade--never an attraction in and of itself. The attraction for trade lies in those variables for which population concentrations historically have been required, that is, service and transportation facilities. [5]

Third, both Reilly and Converse have repeatedly stated that the generalization relative to trade flow being a function of city size applied only to shopping goods--particularly style goods. Even at the outset of their studies, both recognized the tendency for the consumer to buy close to home those goods for which convenience was an important consideration.

Finally, Converse made explicit an "inertia factor" that reflected the reluctance of a consumer to move any distance in making a retail purchase. Further, his estimates of the value of the inertia factor changed relative to the congestion of the larger city, as did his estimates of the exponential of the distance factor. [6]

All of the above considerations are of importance in assessing the scope of the generalizations concerning retail trade gravitation. Of more immediate concern is that all of them are reflected in varying degrees in the study at hand. Perhaps it is as it should be that most people tend to emphasize the generalization in Reilly's Law and fail to reflect upon the qualifications to the generalization. However, as we shall attempt to point out, these qualifications are of unusual importance at the present time.

CHAPTER II

THE SITUATION [7]

Much marketing writing today deals with the rapid population growth of the nation's major cities and with the shifts of population and retail trade from the central city to suburban sections of metropolitan areas. The plight of downtown retailing is usually attributed wholly to the development of suburban centers, and the competitive strategies of downtown institutions have been based on this assumption. These strategies have involved either the building of suburban branches or efforts to rejuvenate the downtown area in order to pull shoppers in from the suburbs. The findings of this study substantiate the observed loss of trade by the central business district. However, we find that the strategy of attempting to correct or reverse the decline by concentrating solely on the suburban movement is an incomplete one. For this strategy to be completely sound, it must be assumed that retail trade concentrations in the combination of major cities and their suburbs have paralleled concentrations of population in these areas, and that trade has merely shifted from the central city to the suburb. Such an assumption is incorrect. Therefore it is our contention that a strategy on the part of the downtown merchant of adjusting to suburban development is inadequate in that it is not based on a complete picture of a long-term trend of retail trade flows relative to population movement.

The actual fact is that during the past thirty years retail trade has not shifted to metropolitan areas at anything like the same rate as population. In other words, while the population of the Standard Metropolitan Statistical Areas has increased rapidly both in absolute terms and in share of the national total, metropolitan retail sales have made gains in absolute terms, but have not increased their share of the nation's total at all. Analysis of population and retail sales data for the 42 states containing one or more Standard Metropolitan Statistical Areas in 1963 reveals the following: (1) the metropolitan areas increased their population share from 53.7 percent in 1929 to 62.86

5

percent in 1963, and (2) the metropolitan share of retail trade remained almost constant, amounting to 68 percent in 1929 and 67.4 percent in 1963. In other words, per capita retail sales have been rising much more rapidly in non-metropolitan than in metropolitan areas.

DESCRIPTION OF METHOD

Some explanation at this point may make this discussion more understandable. The Bureau of the Census defines a Standard Metropolitan Statistical Area as being made up of one or more highly urbanized counties containing at least one central city of 50,000 or more inhabitants. Comparison of SMSA's over time is complicated by the fact that their number increases from year to year and that their geographical areas are sometimes enlarged by adding adjacent counties as they become more urban in character. Between 1950 and 1960 alone the number of SMSA's increased from 168 to 212. Consequently, any statistical analysis of the nation's SMSA's over time must adjust for the changes in their number and composition.

In the case of this study, the SMSA's were stabilized at the number and composition of those which existed in 1958, the year for which the most recent Census of Business had been taken at the time of this study. Data for previous census years and for 1963 were then built up by reconstituting the SMSA's statistically from published county data. Once this was done, SMSA data were compared with those for the remainder of each state. The basic results are summarized in Tables 1, 2, and 3, which contain data on the 42 states that had one or more population centers designated as SMSA's in 1958.

METROPOLITAN AREA POPULATION SHARES

Using the 42 states that had one or more population centers designated as SMSA's in 1958, Table 1 shows the proportions of each state's population living in its metropolitan areas during each Census of Business year from 1929 to 1963. While it will be noted that for the 42 states as a whole the degree of population concentration increased steadily throughout the period, the degree in some states increased rapidly and in others little or not at all.

Those states in which metropolitan area population shares have increased most are generally those that had low metropolitan area concentrations to begin with. In most cases they are states whose

TABLE 1

PERCENTAGES OF STATE POPULATIONS CONCENTRATED IN SMSA'S
FOR 42 STATES, 1929-1963

SMSA	1929	1939	1948	1954	1958	1963
Alabama	27.59	29.00	33.67	36.32	36.77	39.48
Arizona	46.64	51.49	61.49	67.53	70.34	69.38
Arkansas	10.82	11.15	13.17	15.03	16.49	17.45
California	83.39	83.96	84.37	85.50	86.27	85.11
Colorado	43.35	45.56	52.51	56.13	58.62	58.74
Connecticut	66.67	66.76	66.91	66.29	65.74	67.84
Delaware	67.45	67.39	68.56	68.84	68.86	70.17
Florida	47.27	52.95	56.98	58.25	58.66	58.53
Georgia	27.77	30.95	36.29	40.35	42.98	45.27
Illinois	69.92	70.50	72.81	74.58	75.71	79.11
Indiana	43.96	45.39	47.81	49.40	50.35	53.41
Iowa	25.49	26.82	29.10	31.44	32.29	34.45
Kansas	20.92	22.70	23.73	29.64	34.77	41.40
Kentucky	24.98	24.74	27.95	30.95	33.12	35.31
Louisiana	34.29	34.83	38.66	40.76	41.84	43.18
Maine	19.64	19.94	20.49	20.28	19.97	21.97
Maryland	69.90	71.73	71.54	76.59	77.63	79.77
Massachusetts	88.31	86.08	86.10	85.76	85.37	87.51
Michigan	67.95	68.80	71.00	72.19	72.83	74.81
Minnesota	35.02	41.36	45.47	47.57	49.43	52.02
Mississippi	4.14	4.85	6.20	7.36	8.20	8.76
Missouri	47.97	48.63	52.62	55.52	56.87	60.27
Nebraska	24.77	27.04	30.60	33.96	36.77	38.64
New Hampshire	17.51	16.82	17.66	17.69	17.53	18.06
New Jersey	84.69	84.21	82.75	80.73	79.29	77.71
New Mexico	10.68	12.86	20.02	24.36	26.63	27.49
New York	84.34	85.04	85.29	85.42	85.49	83.93
North Carolina	19.66	20.41	21.79	23.13	24.09	24.91
Ohio	65.70	65.83	68.04	68.92	69.25	66.64
Oklahoma	20.19	22.14	28.10	32.78	35.86	40.42
Oregon	43.47	41.61	40.83	40.82	40.90	41.66
Pennsylvania	74.89	75.23	76.21	76.95	77.44	79.22

TABLE 1

PERCENTAGES OF STATE POPULATIONS CONCENTRATED IN SMSA'S
FOR 42 STATES, 1929-1963 (cont.)

SMSA	1929	1939	1948	1954	1958	1963
Rhode Island	90.63	88.70	88.40	87.76	87.45	85.99
South Carolina	22.29	25.69	26.43	29.15	31.06	33.29
South Dakota	7.28	8.80	10.49	11.91	12.03	12.38
Tennessee	33.81	35.61	40.04	42.88	44.65	46.47
Texas	36.64	40.32	48.35	53.35	56.21	57.96
Utah	48.19	48.74	51.46	53.58	54.87	54.37
Virginia	35.62	34.23	42.40	46.79	49.16	50.52
Washington	57.36	57.07	58.65	61.37	62.57	62.72
West Virginia	25.53	26.19	27.45	28.89	30.13	32.67
Wisconsin	39.06	39.75	41.91	44.05	45.53	47.79
SMSA's of 42 states	53.75	54.83	57.89	60.19	61.55	62.86

Source: Developed from United States Census data.

economies, prior to World War II, were largely oriented toward agriculture; also most of them are located west of the Mississippi River. In twelve states, Arizona, Arkansas, Georgia, Kansas, Kentucky, Mississippi, Nebraska, New Mexico, Oklahoma, South Dakota, Texas, and Virginia, metropolitan areas increased their population shares by at least one-third from 1939 to 1963. Eight of them lie west of the Mississippi, and all were predominantly agricultural before the war.

There are also eleven states in which metropolitan area population shares increased by one-twentieth or less during the same period. These are California, Connecticut, Delaware, Maine, Massachusetts, New Hampshire, New Jersey, New York, Oregon, Pennsylvania, and Rhode Island. Nine of these lie east of the Mississippi, and are generally in a rather mature state of economic growth. California and Oregon are mavericks which defy any generalization about the rest.

SHARES OF RETAIL SALES

Table 2 shows the SMSA shares of state retail sales for each of the Census of Business years. Here, too, there is a great deal of

TABLE 2

PERCENTAGES OF STATE RETAIL SALES CONCENTRATED IN SMSA'S
FOR 42 STATES, 1929-1963

SMSA	1929	1939	1948	1954	1958	1963
Alabama	46.79	48.34	48.22	47.75	47.65	45.31
Arizona	52.83	58.82	67.98	69.52	72.39	75.99
Arkansas	18.03	22.75	22.28	22.95	24.48	23.75
California	86.06	85.76	85.42	86.45	87.22	87.32
Colorado	54.29	57.01	56.70	60.36	61.87	62.96
Connecticut	68.48	68.39	67.65	71.91	68.69	66.70
Delaware*	75.66	70.98	62.11	67.65	67.46	72.01
Florida	68.97	66.16	66.34	62.89	63.20	60.67
Georgia	51.21	52.35	52.70	53.93	54.50	54.51
Illinois	80.65	79.21	77.48	80.49	79.29	76.96
Indiana	55.52	54.58	53.96	54.25	54.94	54.60
Iowa	33.91	34.53	34.18	33.48	34.93	34.78
Kansas	23.73	28.39	27.57	34.10	36.11	36.66
Kentucky	45.92	45.17	44.47	46.38	45.63	44.50
Louisiana	51.17	53.21	50.51	52.15	52.31	51.00
Maine	29.31	27.89	26.75	26.19	25.89	25.04
Maryland	77.38	77.53	75.89	76.56	78.38	79.33
Massachusetts	89.00	85.39	86.78	87.38	87.75	85.32
Michigan	76.20	74.86	75.02	76.19	75.16	75.97
Minnesota	55.74	55.29	51.16	52.14	53.77	54.21
Mississippi	8.54	11.32	11.18	12.25	14.27	12.91
Missouri	68.31	67.52	65.11	65.16	64.98	63.64
Nebraska	31.36	37.94	33.99	35.81	37.97	38.30
New Hampshire	21.04	18.42	19.01	18.31	19.05	22.64
New Jersey	84.18	83.66	81.53	80.57	79.54	78.04
New Mexico	17.50	20.14	25.58	29.75	31.72	33.22
New York	87.52	87.02	86.29	85.81	86.15	86.21
North Carolina	33.22	33.98	33.11	32.35	33.75	32.70
Ohio	73.96	74.12	73.06	72.56	73.18	73.18
Oklahoma	31.93	36.25	37.85	41.50	43.69	45.42
Oregon	51.28	48.07	44.70	43.23	43.40	43.79
Pennsylvania	82.83	80.46	79.65	80.44	80.61	80.29

TABLE 2

PERCENTAGES OF STATE RETAIL SALES CONCENTRATED IN SMSA'S
FOR 42 STATES, 1929-1963 (cont.)

SMSA	1929	1939	1948	1954	1958	1963
Rhode Island*	90.45	86.87	86.74	83.78	85.53	97.19
South Carolina	33.81	34.89	35.19	37.47	38.17	38.10
South Dakota	11.62	15.41	14.16	14.64	15.59	15.76
Tennessee	59.09	58.93	57.27	56.96	57.73	55.19
Texas	51.37	54.96	57.43	59.68	61.42	62.70
Utah	65.44	62.78	59.29	62.85	62.35	65.51
Virginia	39.94	42.21	52.76	55.64	60.37	59.40
Washington	64.03	62.84	60.68	63.52	65.17	65.25
West Virginia	36.18	35.99	34.93	38.54	38.69	38.20
Wisconsin	48.00	49.00	46.06	47.46	48.33	46.69
SMSA's of 42 states	68.02	67.81	66.08	67.10	67.56	67.40

*Data seem internally inconsistent.
Source: Developed from United States Census data.

variation between states. Generally, however, the changes in shares of retail trade have been much smaller than the corresponding changes in population shares. In some cases (Florida and Missouri, for example) the two changes have been in opposite directions, with relative population concentrations increasing and corresponding retail concentrations diminishing.

RETAIL CONCENTRATION

The heart of this analysis is contained in Table 3, in which retail sales per capita in SMSA's are compared to those in non-metropolitan areas of the same states. Table 3 shows that the index for the 42 states has dropped consistently since 1929, falling from 183 that year to 122 by 1963. This means that the per capita retail sales in the metropolitan areas were 83 percent higher in 1929 than those in non-metropolitan areas, and that the difference had dropped to 22 percent by 1963. The pattern of falling indexes was followed to a greater or

TABLE 3

RELATIVE PER CAPITA RETAIL SALES IN SMSA'S FOR 42 STATES, 1929-1963
(State non-SMSA per capita retail sales = 100)

SMSA	1929	1939	1948	1954	1958	1963
Alabama	230.80	229.10	183.46	160.23	156.53	127.02
Arizona	128.13	134.57	132.95	109.67	110.55	146.43
Arkansas	181.29	234.69	189.00	168.38	164.16	147.32
California	122.96	115.05	108.53	108.20	108.62	120.43
Colorado	155.21	158.45	118.43	119.01	114.53	119.40
Connecticut	108.61	107.72	103.43	130.18	114.33	94.94
Delaware*	150.00	118.36	75.17	94.65	93.75	109.31
Florida	247.94	173.73	148.81	121.46	121.03	109.33
Georgia	273.00	245.09	195.61	173.07	158.90	144.84
Illinois	179.31	159.43	128.48	140.61	122.84	88.20
Indiana	159.13	144.58	127.93	121.46	120.23	104.92
Iowa	149.98	143.92	126.53	109.42	112.53	101.48
Kansas	117.60	135.01	122.33	122.84	106.02	81.91
Kentucky	255.00	250.62	206.45	192.98	169.48	146.89
Louisiana	200.82	212.77	161.94	158.40	152.46	136.94
Maine	169.65	155.29	141.70	139.48	140.00	118.67
Maryland	147.31	136.00	125.21	99.83	104.47	97.32
Massachusetts	106.14	94.51	105.97	114.97	122.76	82.94
Michigan	151.01	135.03	122.66	123.27	112.89	106.51
Minnesota	233.70	175.34	125.61	118.93	118.99	109.22
Mississippi	216.20	250.43	190.43	175.72	186.34	154.48
Missouri	233.79	219.58	168.03	149.83	140.71	115.41
Nebraska	138.75	164.95	116.78	108.49	105.26	98.59
New Hampshire	125.53	111.65	109.43	104.28	110.71	132.75
New Jersey	96.20	96.01	92.02	98.98	101.55	101.95
New Mexico	177.41	170.88	137.31	131.51	127.99	131.20
New York	130.22	117.95	108.55	103.22	105.57	120.97
North Carolina	203.28	200.71	177.66	158.91	160.54	146.44
Ohio	148.27	148.65	127.39	119.24	121.16	136.57
Oklahoma	185.43	199.96	155.83	145.47	138.77	122.66
Oregon	136.89	129.90	117.14	110.39	110.80	109.11
Pennsylvania	161.74	135.57	122.18	123.19	121.11	106.89

TABLE 3

RELATIVE PER CAPITA RETAIL SALES IN SMSA'S FOR 42 STATES, 1929-1963
(State non-SMSA per capita retail sales = 100) (cont.)

SMSA	1929	1939	1948	1954	1958	1963
Rhode Island*	97.92	84.29	85.84	62.75	84.82	563.12*
South Carolina	178.07	155.00	151.14	145.64	137.02	123.37
South Dakota	167.46	188.80	140.76	126.85	135.06	132.31
Tennessee	282.75	259.47	200.72	176.30	169.29	141.85
Texas	182.67	180.61	144.12	129.43	124.03	121.92
Utah	203.57	177.40	137.38	146.57	136.20	159.38
Virginia	120.20	140.33	151.73	142.63	157.54	143.28
Washington	132.33	127.21	108.80	109.60	111.94	111.61
West Virginia	165.37	158.46	141.88	154.34	146.34	127.43
Wisconsin	144.02	145.62	118.35	114.73	.111.90	99.15
SMSA's of 42 states	183.03	173.55	141.71	134.90	130.09	122.13

*Data seem internally inconsistent.
Source: Developed from United States Census data.

lesser degree in 40 of the 42 states, the exceptions being New Jersey
and Virginia. It is interesting to note that in 1929 there were 25 states
in which per capita retail sales in metropolitan areas were at least
50 percent greater than per capita sales in non-metropolitan areas.
Ignoring the obviously incorrect figure for Rhode Island, by 1963
there were only two states for which this was true.

The figures in Table 3 may be readily converted to indexes of
retail concentration. This has been done in Table 4 for the summary
figure for the 42 states. It may be observed that the biggest drop in
relative per capita sales occurred during the period of 1939-1948.
Since that time the rate of decline has been relatively uniform. Equally
important, it shows no evidence of slowing down.

While there is a high degree of consistency in the direction of
change in the various states, there is a wide spread in magnitudes of
change. For instance, while the metropolitan areas of Mississippi
and Utah had indexes of 150 or more in 1963, those of Connecticut,
Illinois, Kansas, Maryland, Massachusetts, Nebraska, and Wisconsin
were 100 or less. As interesting as these variations are, however,

TABLE 4

INDEX OF PER CAPITA RETAIL SALES CONCENTRATION IN SMSA'S FOR
42 STATES, SELECTED YEARS

(Summary figures from Table 3 expressed relative to base year, 1958 = 100)

Per Capita Retail Sales Concentration in SMSA's
Relative to Non-SMSA's (from Table 3)

1929	1939	1948	1954	1958	1963
183.03	173.55	141.71	134.90	130.09	122.13

Index of Per Capita Retail Sales
Concentration in SMSA's (1958 = 100)*

1929	1939	1948	1954	1958	1963
140.49	133.47	108.93	103.56	100.00	93.88

*Using 1958 as base year, from above:
For 1929, 183.03 ÷ 130.09 = 140.69
For 1939, 173.55 ÷ 130.09 = 133.47, etc.

the central fact is that population movement to metropolitan areas has not been accompanied in recent years by a proportionate increase in retail sales in those areas. In other words, non-metropolitan areas seem to be doing a progressively better job of holding retail sales and preventing their flow to metropolitan centers.[8] It may be helpful to show the relationships between all metropolitan and non-metropolitan areas graphically for population, retail sales, and per capita retail sales for each of the census years. Some adjustments are needed to make Tables 1 and 2 comparable to Table 3. These adjustments have been made in Tables 5 and 6.

Figure 1 demonstrates the divergent trends of metropolitan concentration and decentralization. It shows, in summary fashion, the several concentration ratios (SMSA's related to non-SMSA's) for the 42 states over a 34-year period. It depicts the rising concentration of population in our metropolitan areas; shows the concentration of retail sales to be similar to that of 34 years ago; and shows the combination of these two trends, per capita retail sales, to be considerably less centralized. The downward trend of per capita retail sales in metropolitan areas is quite apparent.

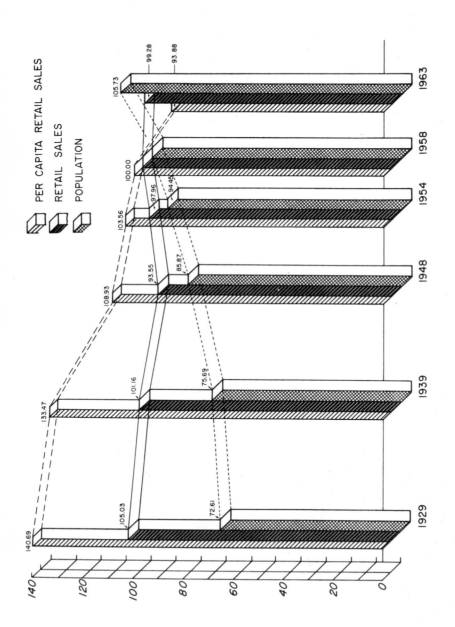

FIGURE 1. INDEXES OF RELATIVE CONCENTRATION IN SMSA'S OF PER CAPITA RETAIL SALES, RETAIL SALES, AND POPULATION: 1929-1963 (from Tables 4, 5, and 6)

TABLE 5

INDEX OF POPULATION CONCENTRATION IN SMSA'S
FOR 42 STATES, SELECTED YEARS

(Percent of population in SMSA's ÷ percent of population in
non-SMSA's; each year then expressed relative to base year, 1958 = 100)

Population Concentration in SMSA's Relative to Non-SMSA's					
1929	1939	1948	1954	1958	1963
116.24	121.16	137.47	151.19	160.08	169.25

Index of Population Concentration in SMSA's (1958 = 100)*					
1929	1939	1948	1954	1958	1963
72.61	75.69	85.87	94.45	100.00	105.73

*Using 1958 as base year, from above:
For 1929, 116.24 ÷ 160.08 = 72.61
For 1939, 121.16 ÷ 160.08 = 75.69, etc.

EXTENT OF RETAIL DECENTRALIZATION

Both SMSA's and non-SMSA's are broad classifications encompassing individual geographic units that vary in homogeneity. Hence there is the possibility that measures of retail sales for an entire SMSA (for example) may conceal as much as they reveal about the individual components of the area. There are indications that this is exactly what is happening.

A study of the eight largest Ohio SMSA's[9] shows that the central business districts of six of the eight SMSA's had an absolute decline in retail sales between 1954-1958. All eight suffered a decline in per capita retail sales (regardless of whether the population of the entire city or the entire SMSA was used).

Between 1948-1954, the top thirteen central business districts in the United States all lost in share of retail sales in their own cities. Seven of the thirteen suffered an actual decline in retail sales. During this period (and since) all of the thirteen cities were losing trade relative to their individual SMSA's.[10]

TABLE 6

INDEX OF RETAIL SALES CONCENTRATION IN SMSA'S
FOR 42 STATES, SELECTED YEARS

(Percent of retail sales in SMSA's ÷ percent of retail sales in
non-SMSA's; each year then expressed relative to base year, 1958 = 100)

Retail Sales Concentration in SMSA's Relative to Non-SMSA's					
1929	1939	1948	1954	1958	1963
218.95	210.66	194.81	203.98	208.24	206.75

Index of Retail Sales Concentration in SMSA's (1958 = 100)*					
1929	1939	1948	1954	1958	1963
105.03	101.16	93.55	97.96	100.00	99.28

*Using 1958 as base year, from above:
For 1929, 218.95 ÷ 208.24 = 105.05
For 1939, 210.66 ÷ 208.24 = 101.16, etc.

As indicated by the happenings to the eight largest U.S. cities between 1954 and 1958, the situation for the central business district is probably becoming worse. Table 7 shows the serious nature of the decline in retail sales going on in the central business districts of these eight largest cities. Note the following for the central business districts:

1) Six of the eight lost retail sales on an absolute basis during the period 1954-1958; seven of the eight lost during 1958-1963.
2) Seven of the eight lost retail sales on a per capita basis (relative to population changes in the central city) during 1954-1958; four of the eight lost during 1958-1963.

For the central cities themselves:

1) Seven of the eight increased in retail sales on an absolute basis during 1954-1958; six of the eight increased during 1958-1963.
2) Seven of the eight gained in population within the central city during 1954-1958; only two gained during 1958-1963.
3) Six of the eight gained retail sales on a per capita basis (rel-

TABLE 7

CHANGE IN RETAIL SALES RELATIVE TO CHANGE IN POPULATION
FOR EIGHT LARGEST U.S. CITIES, 1954-1963

	(1) Retail Sales Index			
	Central Business District		Central City	
City	(1958 ÷ 1954)	(1963 ÷ 1958)	(1958 ÷ 1954)	(1963 ÷ 1958)
New York City	108.0	100.1	110.4	106.1
Los Angeles	94.7	87.1	127.7	116.5
Chicago	98.8	96.8	107.4	100.5
Detroit	83.4	86.7	89.8	100.9
Philadelphia	102.7	93.3	109.9	100.5
Cleveland	96.7	85.4	103.9	90.4
Baltimore	92.1	81.4	112.6	96.1
Houston	96.0	99.0	123.2	124.5

	(2) Population Index of Central City	
City	1958 ÷ 1954	1963 ÷ 1958
New York City	96.8	99.6
Los Angeles	111.1	111.7
Chicago	103.7	91.8
Detroit	101.7	82.7
Philadelphia	103.2	90.0
Cleveland	101.8	91.3
Baltimore	101.7	94.7
Houston	130.2	114.5

	(3) Per Capita Retail Sales Index (1) ÷ (2)			
	Central Business District		Central City	
City	1958	1963	1958	1963
New York City	111.6	100.5	114.0	106.5
Los Angeles	85.2	78.0	114.9	104.3
Chicago	95.3	105.4	103.6	109.5
Detroit	82.0	104.8	88.3	122.0
Philadelphia	99.5	103.7	106.5	113.9
Cleveland	95.0	93.5	102.1	99.0
Baltimore	90.4	86.0	110.7	101.5
Houston	73.6	87.2	94.6	108.7

Source: Index figures for retail sales calculated from Census of Business. Population index calculated from figures from Sales Management, Survey of Buying Power for beginning of 1955, 1959, and 1964.

ative to the central city itself) from 1954-1958; seven gained during 1958-1963.

No attempt has been made to adjust for change in the boundaries of the central cities or their central business districts. There were only slight changes in the central business districts between 1954-1958, and 1958-1963. A part of the population increases for most of the central cities came from annexing additional areas. Neither of these factors cause any change in the conclusions drawn.

From the foregoing bits of evidence we might conclude that SMSA's are probably experiencing a situation similar to that expressed by the accompanying diagram. In such a situation, retail sales in central business districts are declining on a per capita basis (using either SMSA or central city as a population base), and sales in many central business districts are declining on an absolute basis. The effect in the central cities net of their central business districts is hard to generalize about, partly because it is difficult to find a population base that has meaning for these areas. Most of them are probably growing in retail sales both in absolute terms and relative to the population of the central city.

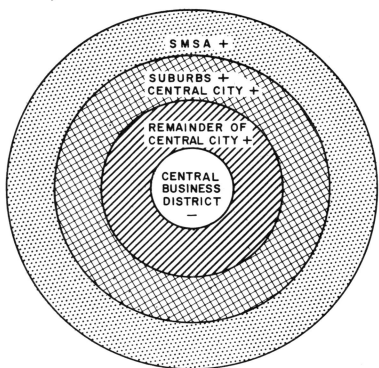

The net effect of these two circumstances is that:

Central cities are showing absolute gains in retail sales, and only a few of them are losing ground relative to population changes.

Retail sales in suburban areas are increasing at a rate greater than population changes in these areas.

The gains in other areas of the SMSA are offsetting the losses in the central business district to the degree that the SMSA is up in retail sales, but not to the extent of gains in non-metropolitan areas.

Non-metropolitan areas are gaining retail sales at a greater rate than their population increase.

There is some indication that within the non-metropolitan areas, rural areas are gaining per capita sales to a greater extent than urban (although such a comparison strikes us as being of questionable significance because of non-consumption purchases distorting rural sales of retail institutions).[11]

The net effect of all this seems quite clear. Retail sales, particularly relative to population, are definitely decentralizing, both from the metropolitan area to the non-metropolitan and also within the metropolitan area itself. Also, it comes as no great surprise to find the chief loser within the SMSA to be the central business district. The central business district is suffering losses in retail sales to an extent that more than offsets whatever gains may be made in the rest of the SMSA relative to non-SMSA growth in sales.

Large City Performance

Consistent with the decentralization findings is the fact that the eight largest cities are lagging behind the performance of all SMSA's, which in turn are lagging behind the non-SMSA's in terms of growth in retail sales. Table 8 shows that with the exception of Houston, the indexes for these eight largest cities are all below the average of 122 (Table 3) for all the nation's SMSA's. Further, they are losing ground relative to the non-SMSA's in their own states. However, there are two offsetting considerations in generalizing from the data in Table 8 in regard to decentralization:

First, each of these cities has a slightly higher index than that of the SMSA average for the state in which it is located.

Second, examination of the nation's smallest SMSA's reveals no pattern at all. Some of them have high retail concentration indexes and some have very low ones. If any generalization can be made about size and performance, it is that medium-size metropolitan areas

TABLE 8

RELATIVE PER CAPITA RETAIL SALES FOR EIGHT MAJOR SMSA'S

(Non-SMSA per capita retail sales in each state = 100)

SMSA	1958 Index	1963 Index	Index Change
New York City	107	107	0
Los Angeles	113	96	17
Chicago	127	113	14
Detroit	114	113	1
Philadelphia	128	105	23
Cleveland	129	120	9
Baltimore	108	100	8
Houston	129	125	4

Source: Developed from United States Census data.

seem to perform fairly well. Perhaps there is some sort of an optimum-size central city, although these data, in themselves, do nothing more than suggest the possibility.

Retail Decentralization by Type of Product

The growing relative importance of retailing in non-metropolitan areas does not seem to be confined to any certain type of goods. Rather, it seems to apply to virtually all types in varying degrees. Table 9 is an analysis of the sales by type of establishment for the states of California, Michigan, North Carolina, and Texas. The situation for those four states, with quite different economies, is assumed to be indicative of that for the United States as a whole. As indicated in this table, per capita retail sales for all types of establishments are growing more rapidly in non-metropolitan areas than in metropolitan areas. Changes have been greatest in apparel, furniture and appliances, and in eating and drinking establishments, and smallest in gasoline service stations and food stores. General merchandise (which includes department and variety stores) is the only category that runs counter to the trend.

Table 10 shows that despite losses that have taken place, SMSA concentrations still remain relatively high in general merchandise, apparel, furniture and appliances, and eating and drinking establishments. Lowest SMSA concentrations appear to be in lumber, building

TABLE 9

RELATIVE PER CAPITA RETAIL SALES IN SMSA'S, FOUR STATES

(State non-SMSA per capita retail sales = 100)

Year	Lumber Bldg. Material Hardware	General Merchandise	Food	Auto	Gasoline
	California				
1948	55.7	a	101.1	102.0	92.5
1954	56.7	128.2	98.7	107.2	83.1
1958	58.1	135.2	92.1	101.8	85.2
1963	49.2	174.9	98.8	105.7	85.1
	Michigan				
1948	63.9	200.8	109.0	140.8	85.7
1954	68.3	190.2	111.2	129.2	92.3
1958	60.3	191.6	102.4	116.9	91.3
1963	47.6	217.3	102.9	123.2	89.4
	North Carolina				
1948	120.1	142.1[b]	150.9	157.3	132.7
1954	113.3	186.6	139.4	135.0	137.9
1958	107.7	184.4	145.0	142.6	137.6
1963	97.3	216.1	127.0	141.8	127.0
	Texas				
1948	77.6	192.3[b]	112.8	117.5	87.7
1954	85.5	207.7	121.5	115.2	98.2
1958	73.4	210.8	119.9	119.7	93.4
1963	57.1	241.7	108.6	115.6	87.1
	Total Index Change, 1948-1963				
California	-6.5	+46.7[b]	-2.3	+3.7	-7.4
Michigan	-16.3	+16.5	-6.1	-17.6	+3.7
North Carolina	-22.8	+74.0	-23.9	-15.5	-5.7
Texas	-20.5	+49.4	-4.2	-1.9	-0.6

(continued on following page)

materials and hardware, gasoline service stations, and food stores. In other words, with the exception of the general merchandise category, the types having the greatest SMSA concentrations appear to be suffering the greatest losses, and those with low concentrations seem to have neared something approximating equilibrium.

Expenditures on Selected Services

It is of interest to raise the question of what is happening to expenditures for services in metropolitan areas compared to non-

TABLE 9

RELATIVE PER CAPITA RETAIL SALES IN SMSA'S, FOUR STATES (cont.)

(State non-SMSA per capita retail sales = 100)

Year	Apparel and Accessory	Furniture and Appliances	Eating and Drinking	Drug and Proprietary	Total Retail
		California			
1948	180.9	161.7	114.0	137.1	105.1
1954	151.3	102.7	108.0	117.1	101.6
1958	144.2	148.8	107.4	116.3	99.4
1963	129.8	136.6	113.9	118.6	103.4
		Michigan			
1948	207.7	181.2	129.5	166.9	123.8
1954	187.5	147.8	130.9	162.9	123.2
1958	161.9	142.2	115.3	146.0	112.8
1963	148.7	134.6	116.2	150.3	113.9
		North Carolina			
1948	270.2[b]	171.6	265.3	192.3	162.6
1954	126.7	123.4	222.3	193.3	147.1
1958	173.9	158.2	226.8	185.7	146.7
1963	158.2	144.0	212.3	134.5	144.2
		Texas			
1948	232.2	163.7	191.3	136.6	134.1
1954	187.0	123.0	170.3	138.1	130.0
1958	155.9	147.0	153.9	134.2	124.9
1963	139.1	143.4	157.5	116.2	116.8
	Total Index Change, 1948-1963				
California	-51.1	-25.1	-0.1	-18.5	-1.7
Michigan	-59.0	-46.6	-13.3	-16.6	-9.9
North Carolina	-112.0	-27.6	-53.1	-57.7	-18.4
Texas	-93.1	-20.4	-33.8	-20.4	-17.3

a. Data withheld to avoid disclosure.
b. 1954-1963.
Source: Developed from United States Census data.

metropolitan areas. Per capita income in metropolitan areas is higher than per capita income in non-metropolitan areas. But individuals in non-SMSA's are gaining income more rapidly than those in SMSA's. At the same time per capita retail sales are growing more rapidly in non-metropolitan areas than in metropolitan. Thus, is it a situation in which the change in income is of greater importance in producing

TABLE 10

SMSA CONCENTRATION RATES BY STORE TYPE, FOUR STATES, 1963

(State non-SMSA per capita retail sales = 100)

State	Lumber Bldg. Material Hardware	General Merchandise	Food	Auto	Gasoline	Apparel and Accessory	Furniture and Appliances	Eating and Drinking	Drug and Proprietary
California	49.2	174.9	98.8	105.7	85.1	129.8	136.6	113.9	103.4
Michigan	47.6	217.3	102.9	123.2	89.4	148.7	134.6	116.2	150.3
North Carolina	97.3	216.1	127.0	141.8	127.0	158.2	144.0	212.3	134.5
Texas	57.1	241.7	108.6	115.6	87.1	139.1	143.4	157.5	116.2

Source: Developed from United States Census data.

expenditures on services, or is the level of income of greater importance? Or, should we reason that the areas not spending as great an amount on goods are able to put the additional funds into services? Or is the reverse the case, in that those areas spending at a greater rate for goods are "consumption prone" and tend likewise to spend at a greater rate for services? The following analysis is intended to shed some light on these questions.

Table 11 is a summary of the expenditures for selected services (more accurately, receipts of selected services establishments) for the four states--California, Michigan, North Carolina, and Texas. It covers the Census of Business years 1948 and 1963 and relates expenditures on selected services to per capita income by SMSA's and non-SMSA's for the four states. Some explanation of this table is in order. It may be observed from column one that for the states of California and Michigan, persons living in metropolitan areas gained income at a slightly greater rate than those in non-metropolitan areas. In North Carolina and Texas the reverse was true and to a much greater degree. Although not shown here, 1963 per capita income in SMSA's was still substantially above that of non-SMSA's for each state.

As seen in column two, persons in SMSA's for all four states were spending a greater percent of their income for selected services than persons in non-SMSA's. This was true for both years. In fact, as shown in column three, this percent was increasing relatively more rapidly in SMSA's than in non-SMSA's during this period. And, for column four, dollar expenditures in SMSA's were rising at a much faster rate than non-SMSA's in all four states.

Column five is an attempt to construct a form of sensitivity index for sales of selected services. In California, for example, in SMSA's for each 1 percent increase in per capita effective buying income there was a 2.34 percent increase in expenditures on selected services. In the non-SMSA's in California, a 1 percent increase in income was associated with a 1.55 percent change in expenditures for selected services. Of particular interest here is the fact that SMSA's showed a greater ratio of percent change in expenditures per percent change in income in all four states than did non-SMSA's. The non-SMSA's, however, all had a ratio greater than one-to-one.

Column six represents an attempt to introduce the relative level of expenditures on selected services as a determinant of the ratio of expenditures on services to changes in income. In this column we are testing the notion that differences in the level of expenditures

TABLE 11

CHANGES IN PER CAPITA EFFECTIVE BUYING INCOME (PCEBI) AND EXPENDITURES
ON SELECTED SERVICES, FOUR STATES, 1948 AND 1963

| | (1) Percent Change in Per Capita Effective Buying Income, 1948 and 1963 | | (2) Percent of Per Capita Effective Buying Income for Selected Services, 1948 and 1963 | | | | (3) Change in Percent of Per Capita Effective Buying Income Spent on Selected Services, 1948 and 1963 (From Column 2) | |
| | | | 1948 | | 1963 | | | |
	SMSA	Non-SMSA	SMSA	Non-SMSA	SMSA	Non-SMSA	SMSA	Non-SMSA
California	64.69	60.47	8.83	7.43	13.89	8.97	57.30	20.73
Michigan	53.35	52.81	6.61	4.79	11.06	6.04	67.32	26.10
North Carolina	49.17	80.33	6.01	4.85	10.74	6.37	78.70	31.34
Texas	40.98	69.31	7.13	6.36	11.21	7.65	57.22	20.28

(continued on following page)

TABLE 11

CHANGES IN PER CAPITA EFFECTIVE BUYING INCOME (PCEBI) AND EXPENDITURES ON SELECTED SERVICES, FOUR STATES, 1948 AND 1963 (cont.)

	(4) Percent Change in Per Capita Expenditures for Selected Services, 1948 and 1963		(5) Percent Change in Per Capita Effective Buying Income Spent for Selected Services Related to 1 Percent Change in Per Capita Effective Buying Income, 1948 and 1963 (4) ÷ (1)		(6) Change in Percent of Per Capita Effective Buying Income Associated with 1 Percent Change in Per Capita Effective Buying Income, 1948 and 1963 (3) ÷ (1)	
	SMSA	Non-SMSA	SMSA	Non-SMSA	SMSA	Non-SMSA
California	151.42	93.62	2.34	1.55	.89	.34
Michigan	163.26	92.98	3.06	1.76	1.26	.49
North Carolina	166.67	136.84	3.39	1.70	1.60	.39
Texas	121.57	103.51	2.97	1.49	1.40	.29

Sources: Figures for Expenditures for Selected Services calculated from Census of Business.
Figures for Effective Buying Income from Sales Management, Survey of Buying Power.

relative to income, in themselves, help determine the degree of change in the level of expenditures on selected services associated with a given percent change in income. The difference in sensitivity between the metropolitan areas (with high levels of expenditures on services relative to income) and the non-metropolitan areas (with relatively low proportion of income spent on services) becomes much more pronounced when using this measure.

The findings presented in column six lead to some interesting speculation. It is probably true that the level of expenditure for services for a given period is of greater importance in determining the percent of an increase in income that will be spent on services than is the magnitude of the increase itself. Here we have a situation in which persons in those areas (metropolitan) with higher proportions of income devoted to service expenditure spend a greater proportion of an increase in income for services than do persons in areas with a lower proportion of income apportioned to expenditures for services (non-metropolitan). At least a part of the explanation for this occurrence probably stems from what is happening in regard to expenditures for goods by persons in each of these areas. For example, assume a situation similar to the one illustrated on the following page--a simple but extreme case designed to make the point. In this illustration, let us suppose that individual A lives in a metropolitan city; B lives on a farm in a non-metropolitan area.

Here is a case in which A has satisfied his desire for goods relative to his income--the remainder can go for services and savings. Individual B, with a lower level of income, has an identical desire for goods because of similar wants brought about by improved communications, advertising, fashion news, and the like--but also because of the relatively limited availability of services in his locale.

Now, we would say that B, with a smaller but more rapidly increasing income, is spending a greater percent of his income for goods. In census classification, these expenditures would be tabulated as sales of retail establishments. Individual A is probably spending a substantial portion of his remaining $1,000 for services. B cannot spend as much for services as can A because of B's lower level of income, even though B's change in expenditure relative to income may exceed A's. Undoubtedly, the magnitude of that change in income had some effect on the level and pattern of expenditures of both A and B. But it seems likely that the level of income (which is reflected in the level of expenditures for services relative to income) had a greater

	Time T_0			Time T_1				
Individual	Income	Expenditures for Goods	Percent of Income Spent for Goods	Income	Change in Income	Expenditures for Goods	Percent of Income Spent for Goods	Percent of Change in Income Spent for Goods
A	$1,000	$500	50%	$2,000	$1,000	$1,000	50%	50%
B	500	400	80	1,600	1,000	1,000	62.5	54.5

effect, assuming (1) that the desire for goods is similar, (2) that expenditures for services are residual expenditures to some degree, and (3) that such expenditures are some function of the availability of services.

Additionally, we are not necessarily dealing with consumption expenditures by persons living in the area in which the measurements are made, but rather with receipts and sales of establishments in those areas. Therefore, we could have a situation in which A is not really spending much more for services than is B. Instead B is forced to buy a good portion of his services in the city because of the factor of availability. On the other hand, he may be able to buy his goods in his own area because of more nearly equalized availability of goods. It would not be unreasonable to expect the large central cities of the SMSA to dominate not only their own metropolitan area in regard to services but also to pull more heavily from nearby non-SMSA's for service sales than they do for sales of goods. The pulling power of business services (classified in selected services), hotels, and amusements should give the city some advantage in this respect--although, as will be pointed out later, the city may well be losing some of this attraction.

The whole question of the relationship between income and service expenditure seems to be sufficiently important to warrant some further attention. Table 12 shows the pairings of Per Capita Effective Buying Income and percent of PCEBI spent for selected services for both SMSA's and non-SMSA's for the four states (California, Michigan, North Carolina, and Texas) for 1948 and 1963. In order to determine the extent of the relationship between levels of PCEBI and percent of PCEBI spent on selected services, a straight line correlation was run between the two series of data. A coefficient of correlation (r) of .93 was found. This is a highly significant correlation with a relatively small standard error. Thus the conclusion is drawn that for these data the higher the level of income, whether SMSA or non-SMSA, the greater the relative expenditure on selected services.

The sixteen pairings in Table 12 represent the appropriate figures for the four states for the two types of areas (SMSA's and non-SMSA's) for the two years 1948 and 1963. These items are ranked on the basis of PCEBI with states, years, and metropolitan and non-metropolitan areas interspersed.

Restating our earlier finding, a partial explanation for the slower growth in per capita retail sales in metropolitan areas is found in the

TABLE 12

PER CAPITA EFFECTIVE BUYING INCOME (PCEBI) AND PERCENT OF PCEBI
SPENT FOR SELECTED SERVICES, SMSA'S AND NON-SMSA'S
CALIFORNIA, MICHIGAN, NORTH CAROLINA, AND TEXAS
1948 AND 1963

PCEBI	Percent of PCEBI Spent for Selected Services
$2,612	13.89
2,160	10.74
2,030	8.97
2,016	11.21
2,002	11.06
1,820	6.04
1,586	8.83
1,517	7.65
1,482	6.61
1,448	6.01
1,430	7.13
1,412	6.37
1,265	7.43
1,191	4.79
896	6.36
783	4.85

Sources: Figures for Expenditures for Selected Services calculated from Census of Business. Figures for Effective Buying Income from Sales Management, Survey of Buying Power.

greater percent of income devoted to expenditures for services, such expenditures being directly associated with the higher levels of per capita income in the SMSA's.

Some Qualifications to the Use of Measures of Selected Services

It should be noted that expenditures for selected services is far from an ideal measure of consumer expenditures for services. Expenditures for rentals, utilities, private education, travel, and all of the services provided through the medium of government are excluded from this estimate. If there were adequate measures of expenditures for such services for both SMSA's and non-SMSA's the effect, undoubtedly, would be to widen the spread between relative levels of expenditures for services in both areas. Further, the inclusion of

TABLE 13

PERCENT OF CHANGE IN PER CAPITA EXPENDITURES FOR SELECTED SERVICES NET OF
MISCELLANEOUS BUSINESS SERVICES RELATED TO PERCENT OF CHANGE IN
PCEBI, FOUR STATES, 1948 AND 1963

State	(1) Percent of Change in PCEBI 1948-1963		(2) Percent of Change in Expenditures for Selected Services Net of Misc. Business Services 1948-1963		(3) Percent of Change in PCEBI Spent for Adjusted Selected Services Related to 1% Change in PCEBI 1948-1963	
	SMSA	Non-SMSA	SMSA	Non-SMSA	SMSA	Non-SMSA
California	64.69	60.47	87.60	73.53	1.35	1.20
Michigan	53.35	52.81	76.25	78.18	1.43	1.48
North Carolina	49.17	80.33	116.25	121.05	2.36	1.51
Texas	40.98	69.31	73.63	73.21	1.80	1.06

Sources: PCEBI from Sales Management, Survey of Buying Power.
Expenditures for Selected Services calculated from Census of Business.

expenditures for miscellaneous business services also causes problems. Most of these services are intended for industrial or commercial use, rather than for sale to consumers. Thus, there is some distortion in the case where expenditures for selected services are assumed to be an alternative to expenditures by consumers for goods. Additionally, most of the expenditures for business services are concentrated in SMSA's (perhaps 90 percent or more). Unless this point is made clear, the effect is to read into these figures an <u>overstatement</u> of expenditures for consumer services in SMSA's.

Although the extent of the overstatement by the inclusion of business services probably does not begin to compensate for the exclusion of the other services mentioned, at least some adjustment can be made for business services (the net effect of which is perhaps an increase in the understating of service expenditures in SMSA's). Such adjustments have been made in the following tables.

Table 13 indicates that for the years 1948 and 1963 there was no clear-cut pattern in regard to relative changes in per capita income between metropolitan areas and non-metropolitan areas in the four states. The pattern is also mixed in regard to rate of increase in per capita expenditure for adjusted selected services. However, the sensitivity ratio in column three shows the relatively greater elasticity of expenditures on adjusted selected services to increases in income in SMSA's than in non-SMSA's. This comparison of sensitivity of the two types of area for the four states, California, Michigan, North Carolina, and Texas is made more explicit in Table 14.

Table 14 demonstrates that for all four states there was a change in the degree of sensitivity of expenditures on adjusted selected services for SMSA's compared to non-SMSA's between 1948 and 1963. However, expenditures for adjusted selected services were still more sensitive to income changes in metropolitan areas than in non-metropolitan areas, except for Michigan.

Table 15 indicates that in 1963, SMSA's were even farther ahead of non-SMSA's in three of the four states in percent of PCEBI spent for adjusted selected services. In Michigan, SMSA's were still ahead of non-SMSA's in percent spent by about the same relative amount.

Table 16 shows the percent of change in per capita dollar expenditures for adjusted selected services for each type of area, with no consideration being given to income changes. With this sort of measure, the non-metropolitan areas improved their position in relative change but fell much farther behind absolutely.

TABLE 14

COMPARISON OF RELATIVE SENSITIVITY MEASURES, SMSA'S AND NON-SMSA'S,
FOUR STATES, ALL SELECTED SERVICES AND ADJUSTED
SELECTED SERVICES, 1948 AND 1963

State	(1) Sensitivity Measure for all Selected Services		(2) Sensitivity Measure for Adjusted Selected Services		(3) Change in Degree of Relative Sensitivities?	(4) Change in Direction of Relative Sensitivities?
	SMSA	Non-SMSA	SMSA	Non-SMSA		
California	2.34	1.55	1.35	1.20	Yes	No
Michigan	3.06	1.76	1.43	1.48	Yes	Yes
North Carolina	3.39	1.70	2.36	1.51	Yes	No
Texas	2.97	1.49	1.80	1.06	Yes	No

Sources: PCEBI from Sales Management, Survey of Buying Power.
Expenditures for Selected Services calculated from Census of Business.

TABLE 15

PERCENT OF PCEBI SPENT FOR ADJUSTED SELECTED SERVICES,
SMSA'S AND NON-SMSA'S, FOUR STATES, 1948 AND 1963

State	Percent of PCEBI Spent for Adjusted Selected Services, 1948		Percent of PCEBI Spent for Adjusted Selected Services, 1963	
	SMSA	Non-SMSA	SMSA	Non-SMSA
California	7.62	7.19	8.69	7.73
Michigan	5.40	4.62	6.05	5.38
North Carolina	5.52	4.85	8.01	5.95
Texas	6.36	6.25	7.84	6.39

Sources: PCEBI from Sales Management, Survey of Buying Power.
Expenditures for Selected Services calculated from Census of Business.

TABLE 16

PER CAPITA EXPENDITURES FOR ADJUSTED SELECTED SERVICES,
SMSA'S AND NON-SMSA'S, FOUR STATES, 1948 AND 1963

State	Per Capita Expenditures for Adjusted Selected Services, SMSA		Per Capita Expenditures for Adjusted Selected Services, Non-SMSA	
	1948	1963	1948	1963
California	$120.81	$227.42	$91.00	$157.46
Michigan	80.06	140.71	54.97	97.86
North Carolina	80.03	173.24	37.61	97.86
Texas	91.54	158.21	55.79	97.45
Four States	97.77	171.28	55.76	105.19
Percent Change, 1948-1963	75.19%		88.65%	

Sources: PCEBI from Sales Management, Survey of Buying Power.
Expenditures for Selected Services calculated from Census of Business.

The conclusions that might be drawn from these tables are as follows:

1) With receipts of miscellaneous business services establishments removed, service sales in metropolitan areas are still more sensitive to changes of income than in non-metropolitan areas with business services included.

2) Non-metropolitan areas grew at a greater rate in adjusted dollar receipts of selected service establishments than did metropolitan areas between 1948 and 1963.

3) However, because of an even greater relative increase in income, non-metropolitan areas did not show as great a change in the percent of additional income spent for adjusted selected services.

4) The SMSA's (with higher per capita income) are spending a greater proportion of this income for adjusted selected services; it should be mentioned once more that these figures represent receipts of establishments rather than expenditures by persons living within the area.

5) Based on Table 16, there is an indication that non-metropolitan areas are becoming more attractive places for expenditures for services as well as for expenditures for goods. However, the non-SMSA's have not caught up with the SMSA's in either respect.

Finally, in connection with the above it should be repeated that SMSA's are probably severely understated relative to non-SMSA's as places for expenditures for consumer services. The advantage of using selected services as a measure of such expenditures lies primarily in the availability of the information for small areas.

AREA SURROUNDING THE SMSA AS A DETERMINANT OF TRADE FLOW [12]

Table 17 has been developed on the assumption that the relationship between per capita retail sales and per capita income is an indication of the extent to which outside trade flows into a metropolitan area. Using per capita Retail Sales from the 1958 and 1963 censuses and per capita Effective Buying Income for the same years from Sales Management's Survey of Buying Power, approximate sales-income ratios were developed for all SMSA's. Table 17 presents this information for 20 areas: the ten high and the ten low in 1958.

Examination of the high sales-income ratio cities shows that some of them are resort areas. In these cases, the cause of trade flow

TABLE 17

PER CAPITA RETAIL SALES AS A PERCENTAGE OF PER CAPITA
EFFECTIVE BUYING INCOME

High Cities (in 1958)	Percentage		Low Cities (in 1958)	Percentage	
	1958	1963		1958	1963
Fort Smith, Arkansas	101.5	101.7	Jersey City, N.J.	51.5	52.4
Laredo, Texas	100.1	116.5	Lorain-Elyria, Ohio	51.5	56.4
West Palm Beach, Fla.	94.6	81.3	Champaign-Urbana, Ill.	52.7	59.8
Lexington, Ky.	89.5	76.7	Paterson, Clifton, Passaic, N.J.	54.8	53.0
Jackson, Miss.	89.4	67.2	South Bend, Ind.	55.4	59.8
Asheville, N.C.	87.0	75.6	Columbus, Ga.	55.6	58.5
Chattanooga, Tenn.	85.8	68.5	Steubenville-Weirton, Ohio	55.9	54.3
Miami, Fla.	85.7	72.5	Hamilton-Middletown, Ohio	56.4	53.3
Atlantic City, N.J.	85.5	84.9	Kenosha, Wis.	56.5	49.4
Portland, Me.	84.1	63.4	New York, N.Y.	56.9	51.9

Sources: PCEBI from Sales Management, Survey of Buying Power.
Per Capita Retail Sales calculated from Census data.

from the outside is obvious. Inspection of the others shows that they have similar hinterlands. They are large in square miles and are rural in character. They also have low population densities and are characterized by relatively low per capita incomes. In other words, these cities operate in rural environments much like those of fifty years ago, with the added advantage of the wider trading area made possible by the greater mobility and increased purchasing power of potential non-metropolitan shoppers.

This can be illustrated by taking as examples the two metropolitan areas with the highest sales-income ratios, Fort Smith, Arkansas, and Laredo, Texas. Fort Smith is without nearby competition. Its location on the western edge of the state places it 135 highway miles from its nearest competitor, Tulsa, Oklahoma, to the west. It is 160 miles from Little Rock to the east and 190 miles from Texarkana on the south. Springfield, Missouri, is approximately the same distance to the north. Within the area so bounded, Fort Smith has virtually no competition for shopping and specialty goods trade except from the four cities listed above. The area is large in square miles. The population is relatively small, with few concentrations large enough to support adequate retail shopping facilities. Furthermore, the population is rural not only in residence, but in occupation and outlook.

The situation is much the same for Laredo. It has competition on only three sides, with San Antonio 150 miles to the north, Corpus Christi 140 miles to the east, Monterrey, Mexico, 140 miles to the south, and nothing but the open spaces of northern Mexico to the west. All the generalizations made about Fort Smith's trading area are also true of Laredo.

Comparing two of the lowest sales-income ratio metropolitan areas with Fort Smith and Laredo provides an interesting contrast. It would be hard to find a city having less in common with Fort Smith and Laredo than Jersey City, N. J. Jersey City lies just across the harbor from New York City and is squeezed in by Newark, Paterson, and Elizabeth, which surround it at distances of 6, 15, and 11 miles respectively. It is no wonder that Jersey City ranks at the bottom of the SMSA's in sales-income ratio.

The Lorain-Elyria, Ohio SMSA seems to have a little more breathing space in surrounding land area, but examination of its geographical situation helps to explain its low sales-income ratio. It has Cleveland 25 miles to the east, Akron 44 miles to the southeast, and Sandusky 31 miles to the west. The only retail trade from the north must come from residents of Lake Erie.

The contrasts between these two pairs of cities help to explain the changes in retail flows that have already taken place, and provide a basis for the prediction of changes that are likely to take place in the future. The comparison indicates that for retail trade flow to be really significant there must be important differences between the metropolitan area and the territory that surrounds it. In other words, the less urban the surrounding area and its population, the greater the relative trade flow to the metropolitan center. On the other hand, non-metropolitan areas of an urban character have sufficient population densities and purchasing power to make their own trading centers feasible and adequate. Furthermore, going shopping in a distant metropolitan center is probably not very attractive when the main difference between the local shopping area and the metropolitan ones is that the latter are larger.

The growing efficiency of the distribution system has brought this situation about, providing consumers with adequate and attractive choices wherever there are sufficient population densities and purchasing power to make viable retail systems possible. Anyone resident in or adjacent to a small city of 10,000 to 25,000 can satisfy most of his desires for goods without traveling far. The small city not only provides convenience goods, but offers every conceivable make and model of appliances, and increasingly wide selections of fashion goods, furniture, automobiles, and other merchandise.

It should be noted from Table 17 that even the high cities in terms of percent of income spent on retail sales are losing ground. Only Laredo, Texas improved in this respect between 1958 and 1963, with Fort Smith, Arkansas holding even. For the low cities, one-half increased in percent of income spent for retail sales and one-half declined. Also. as a general statement, the rate of change was considerably larger for those high cities than for the low.

LIMITATIONS OF THE DATA

Thus far we have described and analyzed in considerable detail the dynamics of retail trade flows in metropolitan and non-metropolitan areas. In order to present a more nearly correct picture, it is necessary to state several limitations of the data used in this study.

First, the measures of retail sales are sales of establishments classified by the Bureau of the Census as retail in nature. The test of whether an establishment is retail or wholesale in nature is the

character of the majority of its sales. Thus, for example, an establishment could have 51 percent of its volume in what the Bureau terms
retail sales and the remaining 49 percent in wholesale sales and still
have all of its sales classed as sales of a retail establishment. The
effect of such classification is an overstatement of retail sales (not
an overstatement of sales of retail establishments). Obviously, there
are offsets in the reverse of this situation in which portions of the
sales of wholesale establishments are retail in character. For any
particular area, the distortions in one direction or the other could be
substantial, depending on the relative importance of wholesale and
retail activity in the area.

Second, the Bureau's definition of what is a retail transaction
is subject to some error. Of particular importance here is that apparently Census considers farmers to be solely consumers. Thus,
institutions selling such items as feed, fertilizer, seed, and petro-
leum--all to be used in the production of crops and livestock--are
considered to be retail establishments. The effect of this interpretation is to overstate retail sales to rural customers, and probably in
the process relatively overstate retail sales made by establishments
in rural areas.

Third, we are forced to deal with data grouped within political
rather than economic boundaries. There is the possibility of misin-
terpreting the significance of the results of a particular area by comparing areas within states rather than within trading areas. However,
this limitation is not a severe one. The county is the basic unit used
for comparative purposes. When we compare SMSA's with non-SMSA's
in Illinois, for example, we classify the Illinois counties belonging
to the St. Louis metropolitan area as metropolitan in character even
though they are not in the same state as the central city. Also, since
the purpose of this study is to say something in general about trade
flows, it strikes us that it would be seriously in error to estimate an
a priori trading area and then classify data within that trading area
when we are setting out to establish some generalizations that will
help to determine what are the likely boundaries of the trading area.

Fourth, although the boundaries of SMSA's have been held constant in this study, we have not been able to do so with smaller areas
within the SMSA's. For example, when we compare happenings over
time within a central city, we are not dealing with a constant area.
Over the time period involved in this study there have been considerable changes in areas of central cities. Most of these have occurred

through annexation of territory which, prior to that time, had been considered suburban and may have changed in designation, but not character, after annexation. To minimize this limitation, we have shortened the time period for comparison when dealing with intra-SMSA data. Anyone interested in a particular area can make his own adjustments for a constant area. For our purpose it was unnecessary to do so because intracity analysis is a small and subsidiary part of the study.

Finally, we are aware that there are additional limitations, some of which are mentioned in the text in connection with the analysis of the specific measures (selected services, for example). It is our opinion that the net effect of all of these limitations may be to change the degree of the trends observed, but not to change the direction of the movement. In fact, it is not unlikely that the trends may be more rather than less pronounced when the inadequacies of the data are considered.

CHAPTER III

POSSIBLE CAUSES OF CHANGE

It is one thing to discover that sweeping economic and social changes have taken place, and quite another to attempt to explain what caused them. In the first place, the relationships of causes and effects are never simple and direct, particularly when several interacting variables are at work. For instance, let us assume that A, B, and C are all related to each other, and that an imperceptible change occurs in one of them. This, then, has an imperceptible effect on the other two, causing each to react somewhat differently both to the first and to each other, resulting in still further adjustments, ad infinitum. In the second place, even when it is possible to establish that changes in two variables are correlated, it is impossible to assume a cause and effect relationship between the two since changes in both variables might have been caused by changes in an unknown additional factor.

Any effort to explain the disproportionately high rate of growth in non-metropolitan per capita retail sales over the past thirty years is further handicapped by the fact that some of the more attractive hypotheses do not seem to be quantifiable and that for most of the rest, there are no reliable bench marks available. Consequently, this section of the report will deal primarily with suggesting and discussing hypotheses concerning factors which seem to be logical contributors to the changes in retail concentration that have taken place, and that are probably still occurring. The hypotheses presented are not exhaustive. They are grouped under the headings of "Institutional" and "Consumer" for convenience of discussion. Their order of presentation does not represent a ranking of possible validity or importance.

INSTITUTIONAL

The growing efficiency of the distribution system has made it possible to provide the consumer with adequate and attractive assortments of many types of goods in relatively small population centers. Much of the credit for this improvement must go to the non-metropolitan retailers who have professionalized and revitalized their operations during the last generation. It seems logical that the extension of chain store operations into every trading center of any significance has played an important role in this development. It has come about not only through the chains' own efficiency but also through the efficiency of their independent competitors resulting from the competitive pressure exerted on them by the chains. The term efficiency is not used here solely in connection with low selling costs, but also relates to non-metropolitan retailers' apparent ability to supply most of the desires of local inhabitants to the extent that shoppers do not find it worthwhile to make the effort necessary to seek wider assortments in a major city.

Non-metropolitan efficiency also owes a great deal to improved physical distribution systems, to alert wholesalers, and to consumer-oriented manufacturers whose product planning makes it possible for them to serve a wide segment of non-metropolitan consumers with relatively small assortments and inventories.

Higher costs of operation by city retailers make it difficult for them to offer significant price advantages to draw trade from non-metropolitan areas. While much of the higher operating costs attributable to large-city retailing may simply reflect a greater degree of vertical integration and lower acquisition costs, economy of scale seems to offer fewer advantages in retailing than in manufacturing. Consequently, the fact that non-metropolitan retailers are only about two-thirds the size of their metropolitan competitors, on the average, does not necessarily mean that they are handicapped in meeting price competition. To the extent that comparable costs are lower in small cities, it may be possible for them to have an actual price advantage. It is certainly safe to say that, to the extent that price and assortment advantages of the major city have diminished, the non-metropolitan consumer has less incentive to travel to a metropolis.

What the local retailer does not have in stock, he can usually get. The consumer, presold by the manufacturer, can order the goods and perhaps suffer less inconvenience in waiting for them than he would by having to go to the city for them. Further, it is not unlikely that a price as low or lower can be obtained locally. Many a local retailer is willing to handle such transactions on an incremental cost basis.

There is some merit in reasoning that the relatively favorable trend of retail sales in the non-SMSA will provoke even higher average costs in the central city store. Every time a sale is "lost" from the central city to an area outside, the tendency is to force an increase in margins at the central city store. Such is the case because the metropolitan store is forced to spread the store's cost of carrying stock over a sales volume that is lower than it otherwise would have been.

The self-service concept has accustomed an entire generation to take on traditional retailing functions. With the move to discounting, the consumer is working even harder to earn a price cut. Although it is apparent that the consumer is willing to spend considerable effort in the purchasing of goods, it may well be that less effort is required to obtain the desired package of price, service, and physical product at home than to journey in search of it to the large city with its snarled traffic, limited parking, and indifferent clerks.

There are things about large cities that no longer attract visitors as they once did, and others that actually repel them. Students of marketing and city chambers of commerce have always known that one of the chief reasons for the flow of retail trade to large population centers has been the many non-retailing attractions available. People have gone to the city to see plays or professional sporting events, to hear symphony orchestras and opera companies, to consult medical specialists, and for many other reasons not associated with buying merchandise. Nevertheless, while in the city they have made the most of their opportunities and gone shopping. Some of these attractions seem to be losing their drawing power. It is much easier to sit at home and enjoy a baseball game on television than to drive to the city to see it. It is also much less expensive. Perhaps as a consequence, many professional baseball leagues have disappeared as city after city has withdrawn from organized baseball. Even in the major leagues, adjustments have been made because of dwindling attendance and gate receipts.

Television sets and stereophonic phonographs allow stay-at-homes to enjoy plays and good music without going to the city. They may also have caused the general public to be more discriminating and to be dissatisfied with anything except the top performances available only in the very largest cities.

The downtown shopping areas also seem to have lost some of their power to attract, partly because of aging of facilities and partly because some major stores have closed the downtown enterprise and developed smaller units in several suburban areas. Even if downtown retailing had retained its ability to draw its old share of retail trade, the physical capacity of downtown areas would not have been great enough to handle the increased number of automobiles necessary to carry the additional flow of people. To have increased the capacity of streets and parking facilities sufficiently would have required so much space that the physical concentration of shopping facilities necessary to draw vast numbers of people from a distance might have been impossible.

There seems to be little question that although the traffic and parking problems of downtown shopping areas cause many buyers to decide to seek to satisfy their needs elsewhere, most suburban shopping centers in the metropolitan areas lack the assortments of goods and the package of non-retailing attractions to exert a great pull on non-metropolitan consumers located some distance from the major city. To the extent that it is true that the downtown area has lost much of its attractiveness and that fringe shopping areas have not replaced the downtown in this respect, it seems logical to believe that the chief beneficiary has been the non-metropolitan trading center, which can be reached with a minimum of effort and time.

Retail selling in general has degenerated, making the small local store, where the customer has access to the proprietor, relatively more attractive. This statement assumes that people trade where they enjoy trading, and that they enjoy trading where the salespeople know and appreciate their merchandise and take pride in helping customers match their needs with an appropriate package of goods and services. It also assumes that customers like to be treated as individuals, and that they are more likely to receive such treatment in local communities. To the extent that these assumptions are true, the customer may be willing to forgo some assortment and price advantages available in metropolitan centers and maximize his satisfaction in his local trading center.

It would be possible to mention several other institutional explanations for the relative decline in metropolitan retailing. The system of paved farm-to-market roads that link the rural population to local trading centers, and local centers to each other, might be mentioned as a possibility. However, there is one hypothesis that needs to be demolished because it is so often advanced. This is the argument that metropolitan retailing has not really declined, but has simply shifted from the downtown area to the suburbs.

This argument grows out of a faulty concept of the definition of a metropolitan area; a definition that does not conform to the one used in this paper. As has been pointed out earlier, the Standard Metropolitan Statistical Area includes both the central city and the urbanized county or counties it serves as a hub of activity. Consequently, the suburban areas surrounding a major city are a part of the metropolis by definition, and the metropolitan data presented in this paper include both central city and suburbs. There is probably one sense in which suburban shopping areas have contributed to the overall relative decline in the drawing power of the metropolis as a whole, and this has to do with their sapping the strength of downtown retailing. It is quite likely that the development of peripheral shopping centers has had a great deal to do with the deterioration of downtown facilities. At the same time the peripheral centers have not developed offsetting attractions strong enough to draw distant shoppers into the metropolitan area.

CONSUMERS

Increasing population and income densities in non-metropolitan areas have made possible the development of trading centers capable of offering consumers adequate and attractive assortments of many types of shopping goods. While non-metropolitan areas of the country have progressively had smaller and smaller shares of the nation's population, it must be remembered that their populations have consistently grown on an absolute basis. Not only have population densities in non-metropolitan areas generally increased, but such population has become more urban in character. The discussion of Table 17 indicates that the greatest trade flow from non-metropolitan to metropolitan areas takes place when the former have low population density, low per capita income, and when their populations are rural in character. On the other hand, non-metropolitan areas of an urban character have sufficient population densities and purchasing power to make their own trading centers feasible and adequate.

The growing sophistication of non-metropolitan residents makes the metropolitan area less attractive. One of the most intriguing hypotheses is that cultural changes have taken place that make going to the city less attractive to non-metropolitan residents. The non-metropolitan resident has become more like his city cousin in the way he dresses, the products he uses, and the way he lives. It has become more and more difficult to identify the rural or small town resident by his appearance, his speech, or his tastes. He has been mobile for two generations, has been to the city many times, and is now sophisticated enough not to feel elated at the prospect of going there again.

To the extent that these generalizations are true, the non-retailing attractions of the city no longer exert the magnetism they did when the city was a wondrous place, alien and exciting, and when going regularly had status connotations. Whereas non-metropolitan residents might once have manufactured reasons for going to the city, many of them today require much stronger motivation.

There is greater conformity of consumer tastes today than in the past, making it possible for relatively small trading centers to satisfy a wide range of consumer demand without having vast assortments of goods. It is probably true that consumer tastes are more homogeneous today than ever before. Of greater importance is the likelihood that today's consumer, metropolitan and non-metropolitan alike, now has it in his power to keep up with the Joneses as far as the purchase of goods is concerned. This ability to conform is a function of both income and information.

The economic middle class has expanded so greatly that a large proportion of the nation's families can afford the same kind of household appliances, the same styles (if not the same quality) of apparel, the same cars, sporting goods, and backyard barbecue equipment as those purchased by many people in higher income brackets. In addition, national advertising and national news media inform the general public about new models, styles, and fads on a coast-to-coast basis, without regard to city size. Such information is also received at the same time, eliminating much of the fashion lag that once existed on an east-to-west and big city-to-small city basis, making conformity possible on a national basis.

The smaller proportion of home and automobile ownership in the central cities of metropolitan areas reduces the proportion of personal income spent on goods in those places. The importance of this factor can be appreciated when it is realized that about one-third of the nation's consuming units reside in central cities, where taxi fares may be substituted for the purchase of automobiles, tires, and gasoline, and where rent payment may be substituted for purchases of home furnishings, equipment, and other items associated with home ownership. According to Life magazine's study of consumer expenditures, for the nation as a whole, around 40 percent of total consumption expenditures is associated with the home and the automobile. The fact that low home and automobile ownership are most prevalent in the nation's largest cities and much less so in smaller ones, however, somewhat limits the value of this explanation on a nationwide basis. But it does help to explain why the metropolitan areas with very large central cities are doing the poorest job relatively in attracting and retaining trade.

Trade flow tends to accompany travel, and people tend to travel from where they are to where they are not. Despite the facetious sound of this statement, it makes surprising sense when its implications are considered. There once was a time when the bulk of the nation's people lived outside the geographical areas that now make up the Standard Metropolitan Statistical Areas, and all of them were potential visitors to the city. With each successive census of population, a higher proportion of the nation's people has resided in metropolitan areas and a smaller proportion has resided in non-metropolitan sections, cutting down on the relative number of potential visitors from the hinterland to the major city and increasing the potential from the city to the hinterland. This shift has also changed the weights assigned to metropolitan and non-metropolitan areas for the purpose of calculating per capita retail sales by geographical area, and has had a definite influence on moving per capita retail sales of the two areas under consideration closer together. However, the influence of the changed weights can account for only a small part of the changes in relative per capita retail sales.

A continuous buyers' market and high consumer incomes have created a situation in which lines between convenience goods and shopping goods have become blurred. Convenience goods have usually been defined in marketing literature as being made up of those products which the typical consumer buys at the most convenient place rather than taking the trouble to visit a number of stores in order to compare the prices and quality of various alternatives. Convenience goods have tended to be standardized and to have relatively low unit costs, resulting in a minimum of risk of obtaining an item of inferior quality and a minimum of potential saving to be obtained by shopping around. Shopping goods, on the other hand, are made up of those products for which shopping around is likely to have a high pay-off in terms of better quality for the same money, the same quality for less money, or more satisfaction per dollar in terms of such aesthetic qualities as beauty, style, and harmony.

A number of things have taken place that have made the original distinctions between convenience and shopping goods less meaningful, or have influenced consumers to make many important purchases with little shopping effort. One of the most important developments has been the establishment of thousands of brand names not only as household words, but also as standards of quality and as a basis for price comparison. This has been particularly true in consumer durables, but has been true to some degree in most merchandise lines where brands have been established and advertised on a national basis. Consequently, a non-metropolitan consumer can go to a local appliance dealer and buy a Westinghouse Electric automatic washer without looking further and know (1) that competition is keen enough and the reputation of the manufacturer is good enough for this washer to be of a quality comparable to that of competing machines, (2) that the price the local retailer is charging is not significantly higher than the price advertised in his metropolitan newspaper for an identical machine, (3) that both the local dealer and the manufacturer stand behind the product, (4) that it is much easier to get the local dealer to install the machine than it is for the metropolitan dealer to deliver and install it, (5) that when the machine needs servicing the local dealer will be available, and (6) that the local dealer, with his limited market, recognizes his need for the buyer's continued patronage to a greater extent than does the head of the appliance department of a metropolitan department store a hundred miles away. The buyer also knows that if the local dealer does not have exactly the machine desired in stock, he can obtain it in a very short time from a nearby distributor.

This hypothetical transaction points up a number of things. First, it indicates that competition between manufacturers, who use similar production methods, labor inputs, and materials, is so keen that their products differ from each other primarily in non-functional respects. Second, it suggests that the reputation of the manufacturer, who is in business to stay, lends weight to the position of the small local retailer who hopes to stay in business but may not, and in this way helps him to compete with large metropolitan institutions. Third, it demonstrates that much of our price comparison today need not require going from store to store, but simply involves the comparing of a local price with those advertised in competing centers. Since the local dealer can make the same comparisons, he is in a position where he can and must adjust to outside competition. Fourth, it indicates that the consumer is not particularly interested in small differences in prices, particularly when they are likely to be more than offset by greater convenience and better service.

Today's consumer has enough purchasing power that he can afford to spend a little more if necessary to save himself inconvenience, and he is protected from making bad choices by the pressures of a buyers' market and the resulting competition between sellers, and by the tremendous amount of market information that he possesses through advertising and other sources, as well as his familiarity both with product classes and brand names.

The shift from home production to the purchase of products in retail stores has been more pronounced in non-metropolitan areas. There seems to be little doubt that such a change has taken place, particularly in rural areas and in small towns, and analysis of retail sales data indicates that this shift has been most noticeable in food purchasing patterns. The implication of this change is probably more important than the change itself, for it deals with the increasingly urban character of the non-metropolitan population. It is a rare farm family today that cures its own hams and bacon, or makes its own soap in a washpot. Indeed, there are many farm families that buy their milk, eggs, and produce in the grocery store and devote their time and resources to specializing in one or more cash crops. Instead of being a more or less self-sufficient island, the farm is becoming a highly specialized and dependent segment of the economy; today's farmer has much in common with the small urban manufacturer.

The increased importance of the home as a center for all sorts of activity has left many consumers with little time, money, or desire for the attractions of the city. The reasoning behind this hypothesis is obvious, particularly to a consumer who is busy with fertilizing his lawn, killing crabgrass, cleaning his swimming pool, overhauling his boat, and building a patio on which he can broil and serve steaks.

There are probably several more consumer-oriented hypotheses that could be developed, but those listed demonstrate that much of the change which has taken place can probably be accounted for by changes in consumer habits, tastes, location, income, and so on. Some additional remarks should be made about income, however.

NON-METROPOLITAN PER CAPITA INCOME

There is no question that non-metropolitan per capita income has increased greatly during the time covered by this study, and there is little question that it has risen at a faster rate than that in metropolitan areas. Assuming these facts, it might be argued that increased non-metropolitan income should have generated considerable trade flow to major cities. The main basis of such an argument is that trade flow studies in the past have found a direct correlation between the level of income of a consuming unit and the distance at which it buys its shopping and specialty goods. It might be said that the propensity to travel in order to make purchases increases as income rises. This probably holds true for the individual spending unit, but it seems to hold less true when it happens to a whole population of an area which formerly was unable to support retailing systems capable of competing with larger outside systems.

The rationale for this apparently contradictory situation goes something like this: When only a low proportion of the consuming units of a sparsely populated area has a significant amount of discretionary buying power, those units are forced to go outside the area to purchase many of the items they want for the simple reason that the total volume of such purchases in the area is too small to support retail institutions which carry such merchandise. However, an increase in the population of an area may be accompanied by a large increase in the proportion of the population with relatively high income. In such a case, the result may be an environment suitable for retail institutions that can satisfy more of the desires of the income classes which once had to go outside the area.

It seems to be quite likely that this sort of thing has happened in the past, and that rising population densities and increasing proportions of relatively high income consuming units will cause the trend to extend into the future.

CHAPTER IV

IMPLICATIONS

Despite the trend toward retail decentralization, metropolitan areas are still the most important markets. As concentrated markets, relatively easily served, the metropolitan areas seem unlikely to lose ground. Rather, such concentrations are likely to increase as the trend toward urbanization (and, particularly, suburbanization) continues. Additional geographic areas will be brought into existing SMSA's and additional SMSA's will arise. The result in parts of the United States seems certain to be large marketing areas of uniform characteristics and opportunity tied, not to one central city, but rather to several. Therefore, we may find substantial zones of overlap in trading areas inasmuch as it will be a matter of indifference, for many persons, which of several cities is visited for a shopping tour.

Thus the trend toward retail decentralization must not be confused with the level of retail performance. However, for many sellers of goods a rethinking of current marketing policies and practices may well be indicated to bring about consistency with a trend that is too important to ignore. Below are some of the more readily apparent implications of retail decentralization.

NEED FOR FURTHER STUDIES IMPLIED

As stated at the outset of this study, the foregoing material should be considered an extension of the trade area analysis work pioneered and developed by Reilly and Converse. In this connection, it seems to us that the need for an entire new group of trade area surveys is implied. We need to learn more about patronage (locale, institution, and motivation) by type of good. It appears that those qualifying factors on general tendencies of trade flows which were mentioned by Reilly and Converse are of increased and increasing importance today. In addition, there are undoubtedly other developments of the sort mentioned in the "Hypotheses" section of this study which need to be made explicit in any predictive model of retail trade flows.

It seems probable that such a state of flux exists in connection with certain of these determinants (such as emphasis on convenience, and changing nature of the central city) that recurring or even continuing studies of identical areas are needed to gain the degree of knowledge all of us are seeking. Perhaps such studies should be of a patronage panel nature. Or, depending upon the frequency of recurrence, area probability studies may be indicated. Regardless, it seems that if it is desirable to predict trade flows with a degree of confidence that will permit adjustment to such flows (or possibly control of them), an area must be restudied with sufficient frequency to detect the patterns of change.

Such studies can be designed to test the hypotheses submitted here. Specifically there is a need to provide more exactness to Converse's inertia factor and ascertain its numerical value under varying conditions of city size, consumer incomes, and the like. Further, such studies should be aimed at measuring and quantifying the importance of congestion. Also there is a need to formulate a more meaningful measure of the inconvenience of shopping by substituting for highway miles estimates of portal-to-portal travel time, parking and shopping time, and discomfort. Certainly under present conditions of super highways, "portal-to-portal inconvenience" is a conceptually sounder limiting factor in regard to trade flows than is distance in highway miles. Although the relationship is quite subtle, it seems logical that under present conditions population is in many cases no longer a satisfactory proxy variable for attractive elements of cities. In fact, after a certain level, population may be a repelling factor. Thus, it is conceivable that the functional relationship between population and trade flows is similar to the illustration on the following page.

Certainly we have not shed much light on the answers to these questions. But just as certainly we have demonstrated the need to consider them as factors worthy of investigation.

The study further emphasizes the necessity for sharpening up our notions of how classes of goods are bought. The distinction between shopping goods, convenience goods, and specialty goods has always been conceptually sound and worthwhile. This is because such distinctions are "true" by definition. But the practicability of using these distinctions has always been troublesome. It is questionable whether these distinctions have not lost all practical significance. Certainly the findings of this study are consistent with the thinking of Reavis Cox,[13] Eugene Kelley,[14] and Charles Mortimer[15] in regard to the

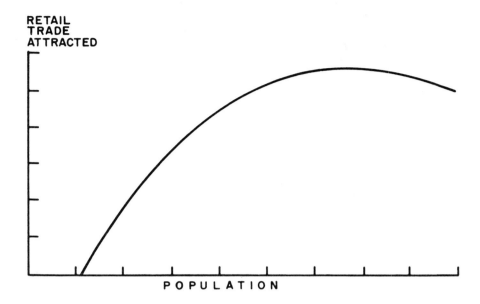

emphasis on convenience, and with the question raised by Richard Holton[16] concerning specialty goods. Among others, these specific questions are implied:

    1) As products leave the so-called luxury class and move toward necessity, do they not also lose some of their shopping goods characteristics?

    2) Does not the definition of shopping include in-home comparisons? To think of shopping or comparison only in terms of the physical product in its place of sale is unduly restrictive and unrealistic.

An increasing number of products are being presold by national advertising to the extent that market control of such products has reverted to the manufacturer. It is in this connection that the apparently divergent trends toward self-service and the emphasis on convenience (in purchase as well as in use) can be reconciled. Even under conditions of self-service, the consumer is able to shop to the degree necessary without the assistance of the clerk and to do so more conveniently by having made in-home comparisons prior to the trip to the place of actual purchase.

MARKETING STRATEGY IMPLICATIONS

There are certain other implications of a marketing strategy nature that are of considerable interest. Those of particular concern to the authors have to do with: (1) manufacturers selling in the national market, (2) downtown retailers in central cities, and (3) retail merchants in non-metropolitan areas. These matters would seem to warrant considerably greater development than we have provided in this paper.

Manufacturer

Recognition of the increasing emphasis being attached to convenience by the consumer may be expected to trigger appropriate marketing action from manufacturers. Those manufacturers selling in national markets may be expected to appraise the real meaning of "national marketing." Any notion that the national market is synonymous with Standard Metropolitan Statistical Areas is rapidly losing whatever limited validity it once had. Those markets which may not have been thought of as permitting profitable distribution in the past certainly merit another look. And in so looking, the hesitant manufacturer may find many of them pre-empted by more alert manufacturers.

Potentials and Quotas. Geographic opportunities and objectives are certain to require constant reformulation. As a general statement, it seems that the factor of "retail sales" will merit greater weight in determining potentials and targets. Concurrently, those factors of "income" and "population" which supposedly cause retail sales merit less attention in geographic plans. Certainly it has been demonstrated that the elusive element of "willingness to buy" is sufficiently important to rule out for small areas any consistent relationships between income and population on the one hand, and retail sales on the other.[17] Thus area targets merit constant reappraisal. And in order to attain such targets it seems likely that manufacturers will be forced to continue to examine and adjust marketing policies.

Shared Outlets. In order to penetrate the increasingly profitable non-metropolitan markets, the manufacturer of durables may be required to relinquish the idea of his products being a specialty in the mind of the consumer in that his brand name is in itself so important to the consumer that its image should not be diluted by a dealer's carrying competing brands. It is not unlikely that such notions in connection with many products have been largely illusory in that they reflect the manufacturer's pride rather than marketing reality. Thus, the manufacturer wishing to sell in the national market may find it necessary to retreat from a policy of exclusive distribution and share with competitors the one or two really good dealers operating in a non-metropolitan area.

In some cases the manufacturer has followed a policy of exclusive dealerships because he has felt that to do otherwise would be economically unsound. In trading areas with relatively limited potential, franchising more than one dealer may have prevented the dealer from carrying adequate stocks to give a meaningful representation to the manufacturer's full line. (It is assumed here that the manufacturer has lost all illusions of the retailer's providing effective performance of the selling function in return for protection.) In these cases the manufacturer may be in a dilemma, reasoning that both exclusive distribution and convenient location are indicated, but that he can't have both. However, it is to be expected that the manufacturer will see his way out of this dilemma. Certain of the practices mentioned briefly below are not inconsistent with a solution to this problem. The point is that it may be unrealistic to insist upon exclusive representation in small cities. And those manufacturers who do so may find that through default they are providing exclusive dealerships for competitors who do not insist upon them.

Encouragement of Order-Taking. In recognition of the retailer's inability to satisfy the manufacturer in performance of the selling function, and the retailer's inability to carry complete stocks of more than one line, the manufacturer may be expected to encourage the retailer in small trading centers to become an order-taker. If so, the present trend toward reduction of retail margins can be expected to continue. One satisfactory solution for the manufacturer is to replace a portion of floor stocks by attractive and promotional catalogues. Perhaps such a program would be accompanied by a policy of drop shipping directly to the consumer's door. (This practice is being followed experimentally in appliances.) If it is true that there is a considerable element of shopping in connection with the sale of consumer durables, but that the shopping takes place within the home and through comparison of advertising messages, and if it is true that a considerable layer of convenience motivation has been piled on top of the shopping considerations, then a combination of limited floor stocks, catalogue selling, and drop shipment has much to recommend it. Particularly is this the case if the alternative is to consider the product as a specialty and expect the consumer to go to some inconvenience to purchase it.

Consignment Selling. We may see an extension of consignment selling similar in nature to that which is beginning in the appliance business. This is one way of gaining distribution in small cities and at the same time insuring representation of the full line on the part of the dealer. A lengthening of terms of sale may achieve similar results to a somewhat lesser degree. Again, the implications for margins seem clear.

Cooperation and Facilitating Agencies. The manufacturer may take the initiative in encouraging pooled orders from retailers in the same general vicinity, using pooled cars and the services of freight forwarders. Mixed car shipments should not lose in popularity.

Service Assistance. For those durables requiring service, the manufacturer (who has already assumed a greater amount of the responsibility for this activity than perhaps he would like) may have to extend his assistance still further. Location of at least minimal service centers, similar to those operated in metropolitan areas by appliance manufacturers, may be indicated in non-metropolitan areas. Perhaps in some areas the manufacturer will be required to franchise not only dealers, but also service centers.

Extension of National Advertising. Manufacturers may find it necessary to add to the already heavy expenditures they are making on consumer-directed advertising in small city media. Consistent with this may go even greater emphasis on standardization, branding, and informative labeling.

In the above context, it should be stressed that many of these so-called small cities really have marketing facilities comparable to those of suburban areas and secondary shopping districts in central cities. For example, a city could have slightly less than 50,000 population and remain out of the metropolitan classification. Yet many such cities have excellent distribution facilities which are capable of providing first class representation for a manufacturer.

In this connection, the sparsely-populated areas are the ones more likely to be overlooked or slighted. The increasing importance of the small town certainly merits serious consideration in the distribution scheme of most manufacturers. [18]

The Downtown Merchant

The typical retailer located in the downtown section of a large central city has probably already adjusted himself, insofar as he is able, to the movement to the suburbs. Many of the larger retailers have adopted a policy of joining with the opposition through the opening of branch stores in the suburbs. Perhaps today an extension of this same philosophy of joining the competition is needed in those areas beyond the environs of the metropolitan area. If there is any merit to the contention that the inertia factor is becoming increasingly important, then additional positive action should be taken by the downtown merchant in an attempt to offset this factor. Basically, adjustments made will reflect the recognition of the expansion of profitable markets into greater areas. If people are less willing to come to the central store for goods, then the central store, out of self-interest, can be expected to bring the goods to the people. One might predict an extension in one form or another of certain of the following strategies.

Additional Branches. The opening of additional branch stores in larger outlying cities is a possibility--going beyond or passing over suburban locations. What is referred to here is a sort of "leap frog" branch store location strategy. Many cities with population between 20,000 and 50,000 offer sufficient potential to support a first class branch operation. The opportunities may be sufficiently greater in comparison with the highly competitive suburban areas to offset the difficulties of control at a distance. The independent merchant may well emulate the chain in this respect, for the chain has long found that cities of even smaller size offer attractive, profitable markets.

Extension of Advertising. An abandoning of the commitment to the notion that the circulation of the local newspaper corresponds to the trading area of the downtown store is indicated, since there is every likelihood that today it does not. Much of the circulation may be wasted with the suburbs making inroads on the downtown area.

But more important is an analysis of the nature of the relative loss of sales to the downtown area. The keynote of retailing today seems to be decentralization of a sort that is greater at the core and spreads outward at a decreasing rate. The central business district is losing trade at a rate that more than offsets any gains in the rest of the central city. The central city as a whole is lagging behind the growth of the suburb. The suburbs are gaining less rapidly than the non-metropolitan areas. This is a situation in which (a) the central cities are not increasing in retail sales relative to population increases, (b) the suburbs are approximately holding their own and, (c) the non-metropolitan area is increasing at a rate more rapid than population increases. Therefore, there is reason to believe that the non-metropolitan area may offer greater opportunity to the downtown merchant than does the suburb. It may be easier to persuade the non-metropolitan consumer, who has already traveled fifty miles on a shopping trip, to come an additional ten miles to the heart of the city than it is to persuade the suburbanite to embark on the trip in the first place.

The consequence of this line of reasoning is an indication of an extension of the downtown stores' advertising into newspaper and TV of the non-metropolitan city. Some of this advertising may be in co-operation with other downtown merchants. Thus in a sense, it may be primary and institutional in nature--a recognition that much of the competition is "extramural" as concerns the downtown area.

Mail Order. Perhaps an increase in mail-order operations aimed at non-metropolitan cities is warranted. Increased patronage from these areas may in fact require a catalogue operation. It would seem to be a logical extension of the service offered by many stores at Christmas time. Thus, the downtown store may have an operation of over-the-counter at the central store, part over-the-counter and part mail from branches in the suburbs and the non-metropolitan cities, with the emphasis on mail order being greater the more distant the location. Here again, emulation of the success of the mail-order chain in such an operation may be profitable.

Special Promotions. An increase in special promotions aimed at non-metropolitan areas with such things as "special days" for certain cities may be deemed profitable. For example, the large downtown department store may have a "City A Day" or "County X Day," in which the store provides buses to pick up at specific points the out-state travelers from the designated area. During the trip to the down-town area the "tour guide" would have an excellent opportunity to inform the captive audience of what they should be looking for upon their arrival at the store--what is new, what is special, etc.,--backed up with appropriate promotional literature. A luncheon with the store executives might be included, at which mutually beneficial information is exchanged. This day could be capped with a dinner and show and return transportation in the late evening. With appropriate organization, encouragement, and attraction such events would seem to have much to recommend them.

Transportation Incentives. An extension into other areas of the practice of rebating transportation fees for those persons traveling downtown from residential districts within the central city may be indicated. Cooperation with over-the-road transportation firms may encourage travel from outlying cities. Such a venture might be tied together with the special promotion mentioned above to include a package form of luncheon and a show--whatever it takes to encourage "leap frogging" in reverse so that the customer would be persuaded to pass up the suburb on the way to the city.

Mobile Retailing. In some areas, a partial reaction on the part of the central business district department stores to decentralizing sales might be to engage in mobile retailing in smaller non-metropolitan areas. The department store could employ walk-in vans with stocks that are miniatures of the offerings of certain of their departments. Orders would be taken from the display of such samples. For other departments, attractive cataloguing and possibly scale models could be used. Unquestionably, considerable assistance in this connection could be gained from suppliers. The van-store could be operated on a policy of same-day shopping, or one-day delivery with orders phoned in after the visit to a particular community.

Such a facility could penetrate even the smallest communities with some frequency. A project of this kind would surely be consistent with any sort of a market orientation on the part of the downtown merchant. It would be an unbelievably inept advertising manager who could not capitalize on the novelty value of bringing the store to the customer.

Mail-Order Offices. Shared catalogue store facilities in small cities may also prove feasible. Here metropolitan stores would share in the operation of a non-metropolitan mail-order office. The stores cooperating might be both competing and noncompeting.

Certain of these suggestions may seem to be impracticable. Actually, many similar activities are now being carried on to some degree. An alert firm, guided by a philosophy of tailoring practices to its market, might find much to recommend operations that bring its offerings to an important segment of its market--particularly since this segment is demonstrating an increasing reluctance to come to the offerings.

Retailers in Non-Metropolitan Areas

It has been our thesis that the non-metropolitan retailer apparently has been performing his retailing activities quite effectively--certainly to a greater extent than he has received credit for. His relative gains would seem to indicate that self-interest will prompt his continuing to operate in a similar manner. Thus, rather than suggesting policy changes, the discussion that follows enumerates favorable conditions of which the non-metropolitan retailer may be unaware. Our statement of implications for the non-metropolitan retailer therefore is not so much a suggestion for strategy changes as it is an enumeration of favorable conditions of which the non-metropolitan retailer may be unaware.

The alert merchant in the non-metropolitan area can be expected to recognize advantages which are working for him and to capitalize upon them, and he has been doing so with apparently increasing success. What are these advantages and how might he be expected to utilize them?

First, he has learned that he does not operate under as great a price disadvantage as he might originally have thought. Much of the disadvantage is dispelled once he adopts a profit concept that makes him willing to trade percentages of margins for dollars of profit.

The large city discount house has not proved to be the destroyer of small-scale service retailing as some have predicted. In fact, in order to survive, the discount house has been forced to emulate to some extent the operations of service retailers with a consequent increase in margins. At the same time, those small town retailers who were determined to survive and prosper either met the discounter on his own grounds or became such high-end specialty shops that they took themselves out of direct competition by serving a small select market. Perhaps all of us know of small-city retailers who advertise that they will match any discount prices. They have been successful in such efforts because they have learned that it is not so difficult an assignment as it originally seemed.

Second, the small city retailer is capitalizing on an intimate (even if intuitive) knowledge of his own market. Here he has his greatest advantage working for him. Although there may be such a thing as "scientific retailing," retailing is not a science. Much of retailing is, has been, and always will be an art. Elaborate systems for information and control are limited in their capabilities. At a quickly-reached point, success belongs to the person with an eye for the merchandise, a feel for the cloth, and an intuitive understanding of his market. It is not necessarily the case that the metropolitan retailer has an advantage in being able to attract "artists" talented in these respects.

Third, for the non-SMSA retailer, convenience is definitely an asset. A substantial portion of the convenience advantage is there by virtue of proximity. But in addition, the inherent flexibility in his operation makes for convenience. For example, it would be interesting to know the number of people who have been attracted by the apparent convenience of opening a charge account at a large store, only to be repelled upon encountering the formality and red tape associated with such a convenience. The large city store may feel that it is already extending more services than it should in the form of return privileges, deliveries, and alterations. But through necessity it operates under rather rigid policies--policies which may be accepted quite readily by the policy maker himself in the small city store.

Fourth, the small city retailer who is adjusting to the market situation today probably expects, and even encourages, greater cooperation from his suppliers in performing retailing functions in which he suffers an inherent disadvantage. Such functions are largely associated with scale of operation. At the top of the heap are financing, storage, and selling; the latter encompassing a substantial portion of the retailer's activities.

CONCLUSION

In this study we have found that since 1929 there has been a relative decentralization of retail sales, in that retail sales in non-metropolitan areas are increasing at a faster rate relative to population and income than are sales in metropolitan areas. Such a shift cannot be explained by the increase in sales in suburban areas at the expense of downtown business districts, for the definition of a Standard Metropolitan Statistical Area includes the metropolitan area's suburbs as well as its central city.

We have tendered a number of hypotheses, each of which is a logical partial explanation of the decentralization of retail sales. Among those which impress us as being most attractive are:

1) The fact that residents of metropolitan areas apportion a larger percent of their income for services and, additionally, pull rather heavily from non-metropolitan areas.

2) The improving efficiency and effectiveness of the small town merchant which make him more competitive with the large city retailer.

3) The emphasis that is now being placed upon convenience in virtually all aspects of life.

Perhaps there is one broad general factor that is basic to all of the various elements which have been tendered as partial explanations of the trend toward decentralization of retail sales. That factor is our universal desire for leisure. Thus, for example, the quest for convenience is a manifestation of the premium placed on leisure.

Regardless of what has caused it, the situation exists. Retail sales have been decentralizing for the past 35 years and there is no apparent diminution in the trend. As a result, there has been a number of adjustments in marketing strategy and practice. Additional adjustments can be expected. The net effect of such adjustments is likely to be an even greater increase in the extent to which manufacturers assume responsibility for performing marketing functions within the channels of distribution, with the attendant implication of an increase in manufacturer control of the market.

NOTES

1. Kenneth E. Boulding, A Reconstruction of Economics (New York: Science Edition, Inc., 1962), p. 135.

2. William J. Reilly, The Law of Retail Gravitation (New York: William J. Reilly Company, 1931), and William J. Reilly, Methods for the Study of Retail Relationships (Austin: University of Texas Press, 1929; reprinted 1959).

3. Among Converse's numerous writings in this area are his Retail Trade Areas in Illinois and A Study of Retail Trade Areas in East Central Illinois, both published by the University of Illinois Press at Urbana, and his article in the Journal of Marketing. October, 1949, entitled "New Laws of Retail Gravitation. "

4. Methods for the Study of Retail Relationships, op. cit., p. 35.

5. Ibid., pp. 21-22 for a listing of factors. Also see George Schwartz, Development of Marketing Theory (Cincinnati, Ohio: Southwestern Publishing Company, 1963), p. 17.

6. Converse, "New Laws of Retail Gravitation, " op. cit., and Schwartz, op. cit., pp. 20-21.

7. Parts of this section draw heavily upon earlier works of one of the authors: Eli P. Cox, "Changes in Retail Trade Flows, " Journal of Marketing, January, 1964, pp. 12-18; "The Changing Pattern of Retail Concentration, " Proceedings of the Winter Conference of the American Marketing Association, Chicago, 1961, pp. 537-66; "Decline of Metropolitan Retailing, " Business Topics, Spring, 1961, pp. 33-42; "Retail Decentralization, " Michigan Economic Record, June, 1961, pp. 1-2.

8. Eli P. Cox, "The Changing Pattern of Retail Concentration, " op. cit., p. 562.

9. Robert H. Myers, "Retail Trade Concentration and Decentralization, 1954-1958, " Miami Business Review, January, 1962.

10. Raymond Vernon, The Changing Economic Function of the Central City (New York: Committee for Economic Development, January, 1959), pp. 45-46.

11. Based on E. J. Sheppard, "The Growing Importance of the Small-Town Store, " Journal of Marketing, July, 1955, p. 15; Myers, op. cit., plus writers' own calculations, which indicate such movement to be more pronounced in western states.

12. Cox, "Changes in Retail Trade Flows, " op. cit., pp. 17-18.

13. Reavis Cox, "Consumer Convenience and the Retail Structure of Cities," Journal of Marketing, April, 1959, pp. 355-62.

14. Eugene J. Kelley, "The Importance of Convenience in Consumer Purchasing," Journal of Marketing, July, 1958, pp. 32-38.

15. Charles J. Mortimer, Two Keys to Modern Marketing (New York: The Updegraff Press, 1955).

16. Richard H. Holton, "The Distinction Between Convenience Goods, Shopping Goods and Specialty Goods," Journal of Marketing, July, 1958, pp. 53-56.

17. For an interesting article in this connection, see Vera K. Russell, "The Relationship Between Income and Retail Sales in Local Areas," Journal of Marketing, January, 1957.

18. Two interesting articles which point out the importance of this market are E. J. Sheppard, "The Growing Importance of the Small-Town Store," Journal of Marketing, July, 1955, pp. 14-19, and W. R. Lund, "Untapped Rural Markets," Journal of Marketing, July, 1956, pp. 77-80.

This paper was produced from a master typescript prepared by Barbara Delprato.

BUREAU OF BUSINESS AND ECONOMIC RESEARCH

PUBLICATIONS AVAILABLE

Books (clothbound)

ELECTRONICS IN BUSINESS
Gardner M. Jones $3.50

EXPLORATIONS IN RETAILING
Stanley C. Hollander $6.50

MARGINAL ASPECTS OF MANAGEMENT PRACTICE
Frederic N. Firestone $3.50

ELEMENTARY MATHEMATICS OF LINEAR PROGRAMMING AND
GAME THEORY
Edward G. Bennion $5.00

HISTORY OF PUBLIC ACCOUNTING IN THE UNITED STATES
James Don Edwards $6.50

CONTRIBUTIONS OF FOUR ACCOUNTING PIONEERS: KOHLER,
LITTLETON, MAY, PATON
James Don Edwards and Roland F. Salmonson $6.50

LIFE INSURANCE COMPANIES IN THE CAPITAL MARKET
Andrew F. Brimmer $7.50

BUSINESS CONSULTANTS AND CLIENTS
Stanley C. Hollander $7.00

THE AUTOMOTIVE CAREER OF RANSOM E. OLDS
Glenn A. Niemeyer $6.50

ELECTRONIC COMPUTATION OF HUMAN DIETS
Victor E. Smith $8.00

INTERNATIONAL ENTERPRISE IN A DEVELOPING ECONOMY
Claude McMillian, Jr., Richard F. Gonzalez with Leo G. Erickson $7.00

AGRICULTURAL MARKET ANALYSIS
Vernon L. Sorenson, editor $7.00

THE ENTERPRISING MAN
Orvis F. Collins, David G. Moore with Darab B. Unwalla $6.00

LABOR MARKET INSTITUTIONS AND WAGES IN
THE LODGING INDUSTRY
John Henderson $7.00

THE EXECUTIVE IN CRISIS
Eugene E. Jennings $6.50

BANKING STRUCTURE IN MICHIGAN: 1945-1963
Robert F. Lanzillotti $6.50

RETAIL DECENTRALIZATION
Eli P. Cox and Leo G. Erickson $3.50

Books (paperbound)

MICHIGAN STATISTICAL ABSTRACT, 1966 $4.00
Also available: Editions of 1955, 1958, 1960, 1962, 1964 $3.00

1957 MICHIGAN TOURIST SURVEY $2.00

SAGINAW RIVER PORT SURVEY, PART 1, 1957
John L. O'Donnell $2.50

SAGINAW RIVER PORT SURVEY, PART 2, 1958
John L. O'Donnell $2.50

THE ROLE OF MARKETING RESEARCH IN TODAY'S
BUSINESS MANAGEMENT
Andrew Heiskell $1.00

OPERATIONAL CREATIVITY
William Wilson $1.00

RETAIL PRICE POLICIES
Stanley C. Hollander $1.00

THE RISE AND FALL OF A BUYING CLUB
Stanley C. Hollander $1.00

PARADOXES IN RESEARCH ADMINISTRATION
Warren C. Lathrop $1.00

RESTRAINTS UPON RETAIL COMPETITION
Stanley C. Hollander $2.00

THE VALUATION OF SMALL-BANK STOCKS
James C. Van Horne and Raymond C. Helwig $2.00

AN ANALYSIS OF FACTORS INFLUENCING RETAIL SALES
Charles E. Van Tassel $2.00

LITERATURE OF THE LODGING MARKET
Frank D. Borsenik $2.00

MERCHANDISING DECISION MODELS FOR DEPARTMENT STORES
Douglas J. Dalrymple $2.00

THE ENTREPRENEUR AND HIS FIRM: THE RELATIONSHIP
BETWEEN TYPE OF MAN AND TYPE OF COMPANY
Norman R. Smith $2.00

INSTITUTE FOR INTERNATIONAL BUSINESS AND ECONOMIC DEVELOPMENT STUDIES

PUBLICATIONS AVAILABLE

Books (clothbound)

MICHIGAN'S COMMERCE AND COMMERCIAL POLICY STUDY
John L. Hazard $7.50

INTERNATIONAL DIMENSIONS IN BUSINESS
Recent Readings from MSU BUSINESS TOPICS $6.00

MANAGEMENT DEVELOPMENT AND EDUCATION IN
THE SOVIET UNION
Barry M. Richman $7.50

Books (paperbound)

MARKETING IN ECONOMIC DEVELOPMENT
Reed Moyer $2.00

PRIVATE FOREIGN INVESTMENT CLIMATE IN INDIA
Anant R. Negandhi $2.00

MICHIGAN AND ONTARIO TRADE AND TRANSPORT RECIPROCITY
Cecil V. Hynes $2.00

THE UNITED STATES OVERSEAS EXECUTIVE: HIS ORIENTATIONS
AND CAREER PATTERNS
Richard F. Gonzalez and Anant R. Negandhi $2.00